HAVE MIC
WILL TRAVEL

HAVE MIC
WILL TRAVEL
A FOOTBALL COMMENTATOR'S JOURNEY

IAN CROCKER

First published by Pitch Publishing, 2015

Pitch Publishing
A2 Yeoman Gate
Yeoman Way
Durrington
BN13 3QZ
www.pitchpublishing.co.uk

© Ian Crocker, 2015

A CIP catalogue record is available for this book
from the British Library.

ISBN 978-178531-033-1

Typesetting and origination by Pitch Publishing

Printed in Malta by Melita Press

Contents

Acknowledgements

THANKS to Paul and Jane and all at Pitch Publishing for thinking I had a story to tell. They might not be thinking it now though. Up the Seagulls anyway.

Thanks to Gareth Davis for reading it through to see if it made any sense. Doubtful. Up the Rams anyway.

Thanks to the wonderful ladies in my life, Sharon and Eve, for allowing me to watch loads of football on the telly. Oh, and for being there for me etc.

Thanks to my late dog Poppy for being the only one of my ladies who waited for me in the hallway when I returned from a match.

Thanks to my new dog Buddy who did everything possible to disrupt the writing of this book by biting my ankles and nipping my knees. He might have had the right idea.

Thanks to my mum who let me leave Weymouth for London at the age of 17 even though I was a naive country bumpkin. She must have wanted me out.

Thanks to J. Whitaker and Sons Ltd for giving me the big kick-off in working life. Thanks to Radio Moorfields for giving me the radio bug.

Thanks to BBC Local Radio for not giving me a bloody chance at all. Not even a slight, tiny, remote chance. Good job I didn't take it personally.

Thanks to Capital Radio, Sky Sports and everyone else apart from the BBC who did give me a chance.

Thanks to Richard Park, Colin Davidson, Andy Melvin and in fact all Scots everywhere.

Thanks to everyone I've ever worked with on live matches. Co-comms, reporters, producers, directors, cameramen, sound men, floor managers, VT, PAs, graphics and most of all, the man on the catering truck who made me a crispy bacon sandwich.

Thanks to the managers for telling me their teams. Thanks to the players for the chance to scream.

Thanks to Weymouth FC and West Ham United FC. Although feel free to do more for me. Like win things.

ACKNOWLEDGEMENTS

Thanks to Anniello Iannone, Gerry Pearson, Alan Taylor, Trevor Brooking, Billy Bonds and John Lyall for firing a life and love of football.

Thanks to Roy Keane – you'd best read the book to understand this last one. On you go.

Introduction

FOOTBALL commentator. It feels a bit strange when you have to write down your job on a form or if someone asks you what you do for a living. I don't know why I still find it bizarre because I've been one for a quarter of a century now. Maybe it's because it's obviously not a proper job.

I'm often told how lucky I am to be paid for watching football and for shouting a few names out. You won't find me disagreeing. It's bloody brilliant!

I still get a buzz ahead of every match simply because you never know what to expect. I've been fortunate to commentate on games that have ended 6-6, 8-4, 6-2, 5-3 and 4-4. Although, perhaps fittingly, I'm writing this introduction the day after the challenge that was Norway 0 Azerbaijan 0. No worries, as a West Ham fan I'm used to taking the rough with the smooth.

Hopefully this book takes you inside a football commentator's life, but it also tells of the highs and lows of being a fan, something you will all know about. We wouldn't have it any other way though would we?

When you've seen your team thrashed 6-0 at Oldham in the pouring rain on Valentine's Day you know you can take absolutely anything football wants to throw at you. This is what it has chucked at me.

Ian Crocker
June 2015

1

Terracotta, Claret and Blue

C ARDIFF City 2 Weymouth 3. That's the answer to an often asked question, 'What's the best football match you've ever seen?' I've watched thousands of games across four decades as a fan and nearly 25 years as a football commentator on radio and television but nothing will ever quite match the feeling when, as a fresh-faced football-mad teenager, my home-town team in Dorset became FA Cup giantkillers. It was quite simply the best moment of my life. Admittedly I hadn't had much of a life by then but it's still quite high now on my personal list of momentous days!

The date was 11 December 1982.

I was only 17 but these are the games of our lives, these are the days of our lives, these are the times of our lives. 'The Terras' — nicknamed after the terracotta colour in their kit — reached the third round of the Football Association Challenge Cup. Get in there.

It nearly didn't happen and quite often where Weymouth Football Club were concerned it usually didn't. They were 3-1 down at home to Maidstone United in the first round and fast running out of time. Incredibly they produced an astonishing comeback to win 4-3 with the decisive goal coming deep into stoppage time. Surely our name was on the cup!

We were drawn away to Cardiff City in the second round. We were trailing 2-0 by half-time and looked down and out. Our dream of Weymouth FC making giantkilling headlines looked just that, a dream.

A couple of burly and surly Cardiff lads had infiltrated our end of Ninian Park to taunt us and they appeared to be looking for trouble, loitering with intent. We'd never really seen that before. The old Recreation Ground across the town bridge in a sleepy south coast holiday resort was hardly a hotbed of hooliganism. Sure, it got a bit nasty when our local rivals Yeovil came to town (whatever happened to them?!), but it was nothing too outrageous.

Early in the second half in South Wales my favourite player, swarthy Italian window cleaner Anniello Iannone, pulled a goal back. He used to clean my bedroom window. I remember opening the curtains one morning to see his face. Awesome!

Trevor Finnegan equalised with ten minutes to go and then Gerry Pearson, another favourite of mine, scored the winner with four minutes remaining. A defining moment in my life and I suspect Gerry felt pretty good about it too.

We really hadn't seen that coming but the Cardiff lads in our end evidently had as they quickly disappeared at 2-2 with heads down and mouths shut for the first time that afternoon. So a couple of thousand Weymouth fans were left in a celebratory world of our own. What a feeling. It just doesn't get any better than that.

The Welsh police warned us not to show our scarves on leaving the stadium or once we had boarded the coaches, in case we were targeted by some of the home fans, a minority of whom had a rather fiery reputation.

The police said it would help that the coach company was called Bluebirds and had that very word adorned across the side and back of their vehicles. Funnily enough the Bluebirds happened to be Cardiff's nickname too. By the way what an omen that was!

Someone did point out that it actually said 'Bluebirds Of Weymouth' on the side of the coach, which was a bit of a giveaway. A few idiots did linger by the coaches and a couple of missiles were thrown but we escaped intact.

Later in life I would often return to commentate at Ninian Park and I loved the passion and the intensity of the Cardiff fans. It may have been a rather dilapidated arena by then but it was a proper old ground with a proper old atmosphere and proper old support.

To access the television gantry you had to climb a very rusty dated ladder in full view of the home supporters. On one wet and windy night I slipped and was dangling off the ladder with one hand while clinging on to my clipboard with the other to the general amusement of many. Yes, well you may laugh Cardiff fans, but remember 1982. Remember the day the Terras came to town and whipped you!

The FA Cup third round draw is always a major event in itself but in 1982 it was even more so as Weymouth had decided to grace it. There we were hoping for a trip to Manchester United, Liverpool or Arsenal. I'd have happily welcomed an away tie at

West Ham as would have our bright young manager Stuart Morgan who had started his playing career at Upton Park.

We listened to the draw with huge excitement and tremendous trepidation. Then, suddenly, so very suddenly, we were drawn away to Cambridge United. Nothing personal to Cambridge United but come on, Cambridge bloody United!

Nowadays they are back in the Football League after winning promotion from the Conference in 2014. Back then they were actually in the second tier of English football but even so real glamour had swerved us by some distance.

It wasn't meant to be like that. It was meant to be Old Trafford or Anfield or Highbury or Upton Park. Magical yet mysterious venues that seemed so far away from teenage life in Dorset. Football really can be so cruel. It was about to get crueller.

On the day of the match special trains were laid on from Weymouth to Cambridge via London but alas these were the days of British Rail. Or rather British Fail. They were delayed, we were delayed, everything was delayed except one thing. The kick-off. The bloody kick-off.

They didn't wait for us and we didn't arrive at the Abbey Stadium until almost half an hour into the game. A once in a lifetime experience and we'd missed a third of it! These are the games of our lives, well two-thirds of a game.

At least we hadn't missed any goals. It was still goalless when Cambridge were awarded a penalty early in the second half but our goalkeeper Kieron Baker pulled off a magnificent save. Surely a sign that this was going to be our day. Naturally we then went and lost 1-0.

A big striker called George Reilly scored a 74th-minute winner for Cambridge to break our hearts. Two years later he would play in the FA Cup Final for Watford so why George, why? Why couldn't you have let us have our day in the sun? Okay, I know it doesn't work like that really.

George went on to have a decent career but whenever I heard his name mentioned through the years I would merely grimace at the memory of that devastating defeat. It took some getting over but it set me up for a life watching football. Where for most of us there are many more lows than highs and for some not any highs at all. And still we love it.

At the age of eight I used to train with the Weymouth players on a Thursday evening and when you're eight that is such a big deal. Come to think of it, that still would have been a big deal at 48.

It wasn't because they'd spotted I was an incredible talent as such a young age. If only.

They'd have been very wrong. Although I did once score a screamer in the playground at Broadwey County Secondary School on the Dorchester Road. It was talked about for a while (probably a whole weekend in reality) but sadly that was as good as I got.

The Weymouth manager was Graham Williams, who'd had a terrific playing career with West Bromwich Albion. He happened to live in the same road as me in a beautiful village called Sutton Poyntz and I became friendly with his kids. So we used to have our own little kickabout on the pitch at the Recreation Ground as the players trained at the other end.

When they had finished training we took penalties against the first-team goalkeeper and he seemed to save every single one. If he ever saved one in an actual match we took the credit for pushing him to the limit. We made him what he was. It wasn't the same keeper who saved that penalty at Cambridge sadly, otherwise that would have been our biggest achievement.

A couple of years later Williams had departed Weymouth but we still used to sneak in to training when Graham Carr took over as manager. He didn't seem to mind despite having a rather no-nonsense look about him. Nowadays, Graham has been Newcastle United's chief scout for a while. Oh, and he has a very funny son called Alan.

While I was growing up, Weymouth had some great players who went on to bigger and better things. They also had one who'd already done bigger and better things. A former West Brom team-mate of Graham Williams joined for a season in 1975. Jeff Astle had become an Albion legend, scoring their winner in the 1968 FA Cup Final against Everton.

Despite a glorious career in professional football, Jeff was another who worked as a window cleaner while playing for Weymouth but I never saw his face at my window. Maybe Anni Iannone wouldn't allow him on his patch. Anyway, I don't think we'll see many of today's top players up a ladder in the future somehow. I'm not expecting to see one at my bedroom window.

Little did I realise at the time that I would later work with Jeff Astle on local radio in Birmingham covering his beloved Baggies. Jeff was a lovely, humble and funny guy who, like a lot of players from that era, seemed more interested in others than themselves. He and his wonderful family used to take me with them on journeys to West Brom games. Happy days.

Jeff famously, or perhaps infamously, missed a great chance to equalise for England against Brazil in that legendary 1970 World Cup encounter. For all the goals he scored, and there were plenty, Jeff would always mention that miss more, the one that got away, although usually just to poke fun at himself. I suppose he had to, considering he could have changed the course of history there!

Jeff was taken from us far too early at the age of 59. His brain had been horribly damaged by all those headers over the years. A tragic loss. Jeff was the kind of man who instantly put a smile on your face. His family are carrying on the fight for Jeff and the Albion fans applaud in the ninth minute of every match to remember a great number nine but, most of all, a great man.

Graham Roberts was a colossal player for Weymouth. He went on to do not bad either for Spurs, Rangers and England. I remember him scoring a 35-yard screamer once in the pouring rain at the Recreation Ground. The ball roared into the goal at the Gasworks End. It might even have been from the halfway line. Graham would probably say it was!

I had dealings with Graham when he was manager of Clyde, who had been drawn at home to Celtic in the 2006 Scottish Cup. I didn't know much about Clyde so went to watch them train to suss out the players and put names to faces. Oh, and to have a cuppa with one of my childhood heroes from the Rec!

I don't recall Graham wanting to reminisce about Weymouth too much but then, in fairness, quite a lot had happened in his career since those early days. He had plenty of other things to reminisce about. I on the other hand could've talked and talked and talked Terras!

His focus was rightly on the Celtic game. Nobody gave lower-league Clyde a chance but Graham told me they would most definitely beat Celtic and explained how in extensive detail. I must admit I was still rather sceptical. I shouldn't have been.

Clyde beat Celtic 2-1 in one of the biggest shocks in Scottish Cup history, rather ruining the Celtic debut of a certain Roy Keane. Chinese defender Du Wei managed the old playing two games in one day trick – his first and his last for Celtic.

The result actually flattered those in the famous Hoops. Clyde had two goals disallowed and missed a penalty. Graham was understandably ecstatic. We'd obviously taught him well all those years ago in Weymouth!

Andy Townsend and Steve Claridge were other ex-Terras who I later crossed paths with during my radio days in the West Midlands. Andy captained Aston Villa and would always do an interview, win, lose or draw. As a young reporter it was always good to have somebody to rely on if other players didn't fancy it, which was often the case. Andy was ITV's number one co-commentator for years and did an excellent job in my opinion. He can now be seen on Premier League TV around the world and will pop up here and there I'm sure.

Claridge was exceptional for Birmingham and all the other clubs he played for. His socks may have been rolled down most of the time but his sleeves were always rolled up. Giving 100 per cent should be a given for any player but Claridge's extraordinary energy and enthusiasm was admirable, often going above and beyond the call of duty. He could play a bit too and score a bit too.

Claridge was one of my favourite players and a fascinating character too. He may not have lived in his car but at times it sure looked like he did. He later returned to Weymouth as player-manager and starred in a TV documentary about his role there. Essential viewing.

I got to work alongside Andy and Steve in their media roles and it's no surprise they've been as successful doing that as they were as players. Being at Weymouth set them up for life perfectly too!

Shaun Teale was another ex-Terra who went on to greater things, most notably at Aston Villa where

I would see him frequently a bit later in life. It really is a small world.

Weymouth played in a terracotta and light blue strip. As previously mentioned this allowed the unique nickname of the Terras even if it looked pretty much like claret really. In 1974, at the age of nine, I decided I should support a big professional league club. West Ham United had the same colours. That would do nicely. Wouldn't it be great to think like a nine-year-old in your adult life now and again? I'm sure everything would be a whole lot simpler and more straightforward.

I clocked West Ham's results over the course of a few weeks. They beat Tranmere 6-0, Burnley 5-3, Wolves 5-2 and Leicester 6-2. They were definitely the team for me and a few months after I started supporting them they only went and won the blimen' FA Cup.

The date was 3 May 1975.

Bobby Moore lined up for Fulham, against the club where he'd spent all of his previous playing career, and at the stadium where he'd lifted the World Cup for England.

Bobby dominated the build-up to the game but it was his old club who dominated the match. Alan Taylor had not long joined from Rochdale when he scored twice in a quarter-final win at Arsenal. I used to love beating Arsenal as most of my mates in Weymouth were Gunners fans. Taylor repeated that feat with a double in the final.

I was glued to the television as Billy Bonds quickly became my childhood hero. He looked the part as he lifted the famous old trophy while I cavorted around our lounge in full West Ham kit and scarf. I could sure get used to winning trophies. Remarkably five years later West Ham won the FA Cup again.

The date was 10 May 1980.

As a Second Division side nobody gave them a chance against Arsenal. Them again! The Gunners had won the cup the year before and in some style, beating Manchester United 3-2 after a fantastic finale. Everyone seemed to think retaining the trophy was a foregone conclusion. No way. It was time for another FA Cup giantkilling.

For Weymouth in Cardiff read West Ham at Wembley. One goal settled it and it was scored in the 13th minute. Unlucky for some, in this case Arsenal. Good.

Trevor Brooking's Header. A Header worthy of a capital H though not due to its quality, more its importance. One of the most talented and gifted footballers I've ever seen scored with a scruffy header. Get in there Trev.

Brian Clough had written a newspaper column on the morning of the final in which he suggested Brooking 'floats like a butterfly…and stings likes one'. The best part of that story is that 11 years later Clough bumped into Brooking in the tunnel before a game and apologised to him. Well, he was probably thinking about whether to for 11 years. No point in rushing these things.

The other major talking point from the game was a professional foul by Arsenal's Willie Young which poleaxed the then youngest ever FA Cup Final player, Paul Allen, as he headed towards goal. There wasn't even a red card for such a professional foul back then. I'm sure Paul's got over it by now but I still feel the sense of injustice! I used to give Willie some right stick in the years to follow!

The legend that is Billy Bonds lifted the trophy again with a 19-year-old centre-half called Alvin Martin one of his team-mates that day. I couldn't wait to see my Arsenal-supporting school-mates on the Monday morning. I mean I really couldn't wait. I went round to some of their houses on the Sunday to milk the moment. As I've said already these are the games of our lives. You have to make the most of them.

So two FA Cups in my childhood years would do for starters, thank you very much. In between

West Ham reached the European Cup Winners' Cup Final.

The date was 5 May 1976.

There was no great shame in losing to crack Belgian side Anderlecht who were rather decent at the time but there were regrets on the night. It seemed a little harsh that the final was actually played in Brussels yet we did manage to go ahead through Pat Holland. Holland scoring in Belgium. It's a good job I wasn't commentating then. I'd have bunged that line in for the sake of it.

Anderlecht fought back to lead 2-1 but Keith Robson equalised before Holland gave away a disputed penalty and the Belgians never looked back. Francois van der Elst scored twice and would later play for West Ham. It was a sore loss to take but even so they were heady days indeed, winning FA Cups and contesting European finals. Where could I possibly go wrong in following the Super Hammers?

West Ham haven't won a major trophy since 1980. If I'd known I'd have had to wait so bloody long I'd have made even more of a big deal of those FA Cup triumphs. To date they're the last team from outside the top flight to win that famous competition.

Some of my mates back then used to change the club they supported to be sure of following more successful sides. Glory hunters! Unthinkable! It's just not the done thing whatever your age. It was always going to be West Ham from then on for me, through thin and thinner.

I later got to know and work with Bobby Moore, Billy Bonds, Alvin Martin and other former Hammers. I also got to work at Upton Park as their stadium announcer. Eventually I got to commentate on my team regularly on radio and television and no I didn't ever break out into a chorus of the club's famous anthem 'I'm Forever Blowing Bubbles' although it was rather tempting a few times.

To coin a few words from that most inspiring of songs, I guess my fortunes weren't always hiding even if West Ham United's mostly have been over the years.

2

Hammered

A YEAR after 'Trevor Brooking's Header' in the 1980 FA Cup Final, West Ham United were back in the top flight of English football and along the way to promotion had also reached the League Cup Final. Only one problem. It was against Liverpool.

The date was 14 March 1981.

Agonisingly, Alan Kennedy put the Reds ahead late in extra time at Wembley but just as glorious failure was giving us a right big stare Terry McDermott handled on the line to prevent a certain goal. He wasn't even sent off for it back in the day. It was a bit like Willie Young and his professional foul on Paul Allen. The punishment certainly didn't fit the crime.

It was in the 120th minute so the pressure on the penalty taker was immense, an ultimate it's now or never moment. It was just as well we had Raymond Struan McDonald Stewart.

If you ever wanted anyone in the whole wide world and possibly on other planets to take a penalty Ray Stewart was your man. Any time, anywhere. One of the coolest kickers of a ball I've ever seen. He scored 76 penalties for West Ham, most of them smashed in with sheer Scottish force.

Not this one though. In stoppage time at Wembley he calmly slotted it into the corner, sending the great Ray Clemence the wrong way. Only Ray Stewart could have had the nerve. The replay was staged at Villa Park in Birmingham. Yes, they had League Cup Final replays back then.

The date was 1 April 1981.

There was little doubt who the April Fools were going to be especially after West Ham did something very wrong. They took an early lead through Paul Goddard after ten minutes. On reflection it definitely would've been better to do that with ten minutes to go. Although even then there would be no guarantees, not with them, or us come to that.

Goddard's goal evidently upset the great Liverpool team of the time because by the half-hour they were 2-1 up through Kenny Dalglish and Alan Hansen. Whatever happened to those two? That's the way it stayed. It was to be glorious failure after all, we had merely managed to delay the inevitable. That would become a familiar story although, usually, we didn't delay it. The inevitable just happened on time.

Such a defeat pretty much set the standard for supporting West Ham United, apart from 'The Good Year' in the mid-1980s, of which more later. I'm sure Hammers fans who remember it would agree that 'The Good Year' deserves a right big fat lovely chapter of its own.

By the end of that decade the Hammers had been relegated and had dispensed with the services of John Lyall after 34 years at the club in various guises. I had never known anything other than John Lyall being my team's manager, although of course prior to him Ron Greenwood had spent 13 years in charge. Greenwood was before my time, although evidently ahead of his own.

Lyall and Greenwood were long-stay managers, such was the West Ham way, although that was about to change. In a shock move, Lou Macari was named as Lyall's replacement but he didn't last long, a victim of the St Valentine's Day Massacre.

The date was 14 February 1990.

You probably guessed the 14 February bit. A group of mates bumped off our girlfriends for the other love of our lives, West Ham United. After a long and horrendous journey north in torrential rain on the M6 we stood amid a monsoon on the open terracing of Boundary Park, Oldham. There was nowhere to take cover and nowhere to hide in more ways than one.

It was the first leg of the League Cup semi-final and somehow we contrived to lose 6-0 to Oldham Athletic. Six bloody nil. Or as the vidi-printer would have said Oldham 6 (SIX) West Ham 0. Just to RUB IT IN.

The only saving grace was the tremendous camaraderie among the West Ham fans that night with a few renditions of 'We'll score seven at Upton Park' and 'We've got a corner you ain't you ain't'. We were singing in the rain more than Gene Kelly ever did. I honestly don't think I've been more soaked at a game than that night in Oldham and remember I've worked in Scotland a lot.

We also kept the ball a few times when it came in our end and there was some high-quality head tennis going on as well as some deft control considering the lack of space on the packed terracing. It's a pet hate of mine these days when fans refuse to return the ball. What's the point? But when you're 6-0 down at Oldham it seemed like there was a point.

I recall arriving back home in London after another rain-sodden delayed journey at 4am to a girlfriend suffering from a severe bout of Valentine Rejectionitis and knowingly asking, 'Did you have a good time?' Okay, you win love, unlike West Ham, and no, that girlfriend didn't hang around for long. I didn't blame her.

We battered Oldham in the second leg. On another night our chants of 'We'll score seven at Upton Park' might have actually come to fruition. We won 3-0 but hit the bar and post and had chances galore. Honestly, we came close but not close enough. Another feeling of claret and blue déjà vu.

We shouldn't have been overly surprised at such a spectacular flop because we had been warned a year earlier when the Hammers also reached the last four of the League Cup. They ended up being very much the last of the four again.

On this occasion it was Luton Town, another team who always seemed to beat us, a fact that led to Robert Banks's excellent book *An Irrational Hatred of Luton*. Only a West Ham fan would understand that title. Well, Watford fans might but they'll probably claim their hatred of their rivals IS rational!

Big Mick Harford terrorised the Hammers in the first leg and our goalkeeper Allan McKnight's abysmal performance led to him being renamed by West Ham Supporters' Deed Poll as Allan McKnightmare. A 3-0 defeat wasn't as bad as 6-0 but it was at home so felt a bit like 6-0.

I remember going to Kenilworth Road for the second leg thinking we were actually going to do it, going to complete one of football's great comebacks which would be talked about for years. I've no idea why I believed that. I might have just been in denial. Luton turned us over again naturally.

To add some irony to the Oldham debacle, some amount of years later in 2014 we managed to lose 6-0 again in a League Cup semi-final. It was to the multi-million pound megastars of Manchester City at least, but even so, a considerable achievement to repeat our feat of 1990! At least they weren't Oldham. And at least there was no faint, false hope in the second leg this time. City swotted us again.

After so much practice at cocking up League Cup semi-finals we were due a debacle in an FA Cup semi-final, although this one was not of our own making.

The date was 14 April 1991.

We faced Brian Clough's Nottingham Forest at Villa Park, where a decade earlier we'd lost the League Cup Final to Liverpool. I know that bears little relation to this story but you remember these things as a fan.

Clough had never won the FA Cup and the nation seemed to be willing him on to end his personal hoodoo. I was a big fan of Cloughie myself and would have been cheering him on too had he not been facing my beloved Hammers, who were now managed by my number one childhood hero, Billy Bonds.

We will never know if West Ham could have reached the FA Cup Final that year. But we will always think it might just have happened. Because along came Keith Hackett. Keith bloody Hackett. Just 18 minutes into the semi-final he showed a red card to Tony Gale for a so-called professional foul on Gary Crosby. It seemed so very harsh at the time. Hackett's decision proved critical as Forest soon took charge and ended up thrashing us 4-0.

Galey couldn't bring himself to speak to Hackett during the rest of his playing career and they only recently came together for a website encounter. Galey has a good story about that but it's the opening line of his after-dinner patter so I don't want to spoil it! I'm not sure Galey has mellowed over that decision though. He had a terrific career and was denied a possible FA Cup Final appearance.

Don't get me wrong, Forest might have won anyway, but who knows? We never will know and it still bloody hurts. I know I should have probably got over it by now but I haven't. So there.

Yet again though the spirit of the West Ham fans shone through at Villa Park. We spent the rest of the game singing 'Billy Bonds's claret and blue army' non-stop, and boy do I mean non-stop. We were at it even when Forest were scoring their goals, drowning out their cheering fans, and we were still at it when the game finished and even on the train home.

I've experienced some great atmospheres in and around football grounds over the years but I'm not sure I've witnessed such a remarkable show of togetherness as the Hammers fans on that day. It was as one, it was beyond special. We had got what we deserved against Oldham and Luton, fair enough, but this was different. Our hopes had been Hacketted to death.

Many years later I bumped into Keith at a function. I was next to somebody he knew and he was chatting away merrily, nodding in my direction, expecting an introduction. I decided to do a Galey on him and not speak to him. How very stupid, petty, childish and irrational of me to blank him. And do you know what? It felt bloody brilliant!

Amid the doom and gloom there were some occasional 'Knees up Mother Brown' moments.

The date was 30 November 1988.

We trounced Liverpool for a change, in fact we absolutely torched them. A young Paul Ince stole the show with two goals and a breathtaking display under the Upton Park lights in a League Cup tie.

Tony Gale fired in a fabulous free kick. So fabulous he still talks about it. Alan Devonshire and Liam Brady were positively purring as the Hammers won 4-1. It was one of the best team performances I've ever seen and one of the best individual performances I've ever seen from Ince.

Paul Ince left the Hammers under a cloud after he was pictured in a Manchester United shirt before officially signing for them. The east London faithful haven't forgiven him to this day but I can't say I was overly bothered by it. He was too good for us, good luck to him.

Having watched Ince develop into a top-class player in his formative years, you know you're getting on a bit when you're commentating on his son! I bumped into Thomas a few times at Blackpool. A charming, courteous young man who had time for everyone, setting a fine example. A credit to himself and his parents.

West Ham were often a yo-yo club, swapping the top flight for the second tier on a regular basis, but at least with every relegation there was a promotion not too far away. We managed to miss the first year of the sparkling new Premier League but joined the big party for the second season.

The date was 8 May 1993.

A final-day victory over Cambridge United in the old First Division saw us pip Portsmouth to the runners-up spot on goal difference. The champions were a Kevin Keegan-inspired Newcastle.

By the way, have a bit of that Cambridge bloody United. They were relegated as a result. Well, that's for knocking Weymouth out of the FA Cup ten years previously. At least they didn't ruin my life this time and my train was on time. It's a good job I didn't see George Reilly about, I'd have given that dream-breaker something back and all!

Harry Redknapp was assistant manager to Billy Bonds but later succeeded Billy as manager. The two had been very close since their teenage years but Billy didn't much like the way it happened. Their relationship sadly ended there and then, never to be repaired. I liked both of them but was gutted to see Billy leave for personal childhood hero reasons.

Harry spent seven years as West Ham manager. He's never much liked like his wheeler-dealer reputation but in 1997 he brought in John Hartson and Paul Kitson in a masterstroke which staved off relegation.

By the end of that decade Harry's Hammers had finished fifth in the Premier League and also won the Intertoto Cup. Yes, West Ham United were 'Kings of Europe'!

There was rarely a dull moment in Harry's seven years in charge and he gave the fans a chance to watch Paolo Di Canio play at close quarters and for that everyone will be eternally grateful. He was so much better than Marco Boogers and Florin Raducioiu for sure.

Reserve team coach Glenn Roeder was Harry's surprise successor. On the brink of relegation a season later Roeder was diagnosed with a brain tumour to put everything in perspective. The legend that is Sir Trevor Brooking became caretaker boss.

He didn't actually officially become Sir Trevor until a couple of years later but I'd already personally knighted him for 'Services to Beating Arsenal With a Rubbish Header in the FA Cup Final'.

Sir Trev so nearly kept West Ham in the Premier League. I seem to use the word 'nearly' a lot in this book. The Hammers were relegated with a record 42 points. It could only happen to us.

Alan Pardew's exciting reign as manager began with a play-off final in his first season in charge, 2003/04. Crystal Palace edged it 1-0 on the day but the Hammers returned to the Millennium Stadium in Cardiff a year later and beat Preston North End 1-0 to make it back to the Premier League.

The year after we completed a hat-trick of visits to the Millennium Stadium as Pardew guided us to the FA Cup Final. Thanks a lot Keith bloody Hackett, it only took us 25 years to get there.

The date was 13 May 2006.

The 13th? Could be unlucky for some. I know 'Trevor Brooking's Header' was in the 13th minute but maybe we had used up all our luck back then. It was probably payback time.

It all started well enough mind you. West Ham led 2-0 and then 3-2 and were seconds away from glory when Steven Gerrard fired a 30-yard strike past Shaka Hislop with virtually the last kick. Liverpool won on penalties. So close yet so far. Nearly but not quite. Same old bloody West Ham.

It became known as 'The Gerrard Final' and fair play to such an exceptional player but why couldn't it have been 'The Konchesky Final' or 'The Shaka Final'? It's not too much to bloody ask is it? For crying out loud.

I would've liked to have seen Pardew stay at West Ham for a long spell as manager and not just because I got to know him and like him. His record was pretty damn good and it still is these days.

Alan Curbishley took over and seemed a natural for the job having started his playing career at Upton Park. I'd seen a lot of Curbs during his long spell as Charlton manager and liked him a lot. I was hoping that if Alan P couldn't have a lengthy stay as manager then maybe Alan C would.

West Ham stayed up in 2007 when Carlos Tevez scored a final-day winner at Manchester United. There were serious questions over the legalities of Tevez's contract but it was a strange time for the club all round. They were certainly having an identity crisis under Icelandic owners and eventually Curbishley was sacked.

Gianfranco Zola was next in the job and there were promising signs for a while but again it didn't work out in the long term. I hope he's not going to be one of those great players who fails to make it as a manager because what a player he was.

Avram Grant was a puzzling appointment and his spell ended in relegation which was confirmed in typical Hammers style, losing 3-2 at Wigan on the final day after leading 2-0. Grant didn't really do it for me. He looked like a guy who couldn't believe his luck that he'd got to manage West Ham, Chelsea and Portsmouth.

Big Sam Allardyce was charged with bringing West Ham straight back to the Premier League. He did just that with a play-off final victory over Blackpool in 2012. Sam then comfortably kept the Hammers among the elite of English football.

Sam was often accused of a certain style of football yet I quite liked him and his teams. I used to love the way his Bolton side set about the big boys. Plus they did have the likes of Jay-Jay Okocha, Youri Djorkaeff, Ivan Campo and even Fernando Hierro playing for them.

A fair few West Ham fans didn't really take to Sam and were never going to but he definitely delivered what was asked of him by the owners.

In the 2014/15 season the Hammers were again never in danger of relegation but capitulated in the FA Cup, losing 4-0 at West Brom, and were knocked out of the League Cup by League 1 side Sheffield United. We sure know how to make the least of a cup tie.

Part of Big Sam's problem is that I'm not sure being in mid-table suits many West Ham fans. They like a bit of drama, a relegation battle, a cup run. Something to bloody worry about. Boring old mid-table is not something they've been brought up on.

Sam was never seen as a Pearly King for doing it his way rather than 'The West Ham Way'. It's a long time since 'The West Ham Way' brought results and trophies mind. It's a long time since Billy Bonds lifted those FA Cups. It's a long time since West Ham won the World Cup for England!

I quite like the romantic notion of 'The West Ham Way' but after so many years of nothing and suffering and enough nearly but not quite stories to last a lifetime, any which bloody way will do for me.

I've almost had enough of them forever bursting my bubbles. However, note the use of the word 'almost'. Yes, I always forgive them in the end of course. It's part of the deal between club and supporter. Well, you've just got to come back for more haven't you?

After all, one day there might be a trophy in the offing and there are three little words that I doubt I'm alone in uttering every year in the month of May. Maybe next season.

Next season will actually be an emotional one regardless. It'll be West Ham's final year at the Boleyn Ground before they move to the Olympic Stadium. It's happened to a lot of clubs in the modern era and is usually for the better. I'm sure it will be for West Ham.

We've seen the end for the likes of Highbury, Filbert Street, Roker Park, The Dell, Ninian Park and the Baseball Ground. Legendary venues but football has to move on, to keep up with the times. I've not quite got my head around it yet though. It's okay when it happens to other clubs but it's a bit different when it's your own.

I think I'll be all right about it eventually but I'm going to have to go and say goodbye to Upton Park and if I manage to do that without bawling my eyes out that would be one of my greatest achievements. I might even have to be there for the last rendition of 'I'm Forever Blowing Bubbles' before Upton Park fades and dies.

Mind you, hang on a minute, 'Fortunes always hiding, I've looked everywhere' – maybe those fortunes are at the Olympic Stadium. Maybe we've been looking in the wrong place. Wouldn't that have been just typical of us?

3

The Good Year

ANY West Ham fans of my generation will fondly remember 'The Good Year' forever and a day. In the 1985/86 season, fuelled by the goals of a lethal partnership between Frank McAvennie and Tony Cottee, the Hammers came ridiculously close to winning the title. Yes. The league championship. The big one.

We didn't win it of course. Liverpool did. That was the way it was at the time.

Liverpool usually did. Although they were actually a long way behind their Merseyside rivals Everton with a couple of months of the season to go. However, after winning the big derby at Anfield, Everton stumbled and stuttered and Liverpool took advantage and put together a remarkable winning streak.

West Ham came third after Everton just pipped us to the runners-up spot. Even so it was enough, more than enough to be tagged 'The Good Year' because let's be honest here, it will take some beating.

When the season began there was little evidence to suggest the Hammers would come anywhere close to being crowned champions of England. The very thought of it seemed preposterous anyway. After winning just one of our opening seven games a relegation fight appeared more likely and we were never averse to one of those.

By the end of September we were in an unlucky 13th place – that number again, it seems to spring up a lot. We were evidently going nowhere in particular and taking the fast route there. But hang on! Hang bloody on!

By the end of December we had shot up to third place. Sadly there was no deal in place for live televised football in the first half of that season. It's hard to imagine that happening these days! So the nation hadn't been able to see our remarkable rise to the top but the viewers were about to join us for a journey and a half; the second half of that astonishing campaign.

In back-to-back games at the end of March we thrashed Chelsea 4-0 at Stamford Bridge and beat

Spurs 2-1 at home. You know things are going really well when you give two of your fierce London rivals a right good slap, although we played Chelsea again not long after at Upton Park and lost 2-1. How typical of us to deliver a daft stumble when we were going so well. That's West Ham for you, even in the good times.

After that defeat though we won five games in a row and come the final Saturday of the season the Hammers still had a chance of taking the title. The Hammers still had a chance of taking the title. Sorry, I just had to say that again to be sure.

The date was 3 May 1986.

We were in second place but we needed to win at already relegated West Brom and then hope Liverpool slipped up at Chelsea.

Alas the words 'Liverpool' and 'slipped up' didn't go together very often – not back then anyway! The word 'hope' often went together with West Ham but was usually preceded by a 'no' or adjoined by a 'less'.

West Ham took an early lead at The Hawthorns with a classic looping header from Frank McAvennie and by the half-hour mark we were 2-0 up after the class act that was Alan Dickens strode purposefully into Albion territory. He found McAvennie who quickly set up Tony Cottee. It was appropriate that those two were already in on the act.

We were doing what we had to do but steady on, this is West Ham United. Things could change. Naturally, they did. West Brom quickly got a goal back and then went and equalised early in the second half from the penalty spot. There was no point in doing things easy. That wouldn't be the West Ham way.

And do you know who scored that penalty for West Brom? George Reilly. George bloody Reilly. The man who had knocked Weymouth out of the FA Cup four years earlier at Cambridge bloody United had come back to haunt me, my life and my personal space. Although this time thankfully it was only for a short while. Beat it George. Go away.

Suddenly and beautifully West Ham were awarded a penalty of their own and of course we had Ray Stewart. No worries. No danger. No problem. Never in doubt. Bang. Goal.

The Hammers won 3-2 but it mattered not. Kenny Dalglish had scored the only goal of the game at Chelsea as Kenny and Liverpool did what they had to do, as per bloody usual. Liverpool were champions. Again. It was Dalglish's first season as their player-manager too, he could do no wrong.

We had pushed Liverpool all the way but that didn't make me feel any better. I couldn't even accept it as a consolation because we so tantalisingly close it hurt. I thought I was feeling bad, imagine what the players must have been thinking.

We still had to go to third-placed Everton on the Monday night after in a re-arranged game. They were soon second-placed Everton, beating us 3-1. Sadly it was even a step too far for us to finish as runners-up.

The boys of 1986 have taken their rightful place in West Ham United's history. The likes of Phil Parkes, Ray Stewart, Steve Walford, Tony Gale, Alvin Martin, Mark Ward, Alan Dickens, Neil Orr, George Parris, Geoff Pike, Alan Devonshire, Frank McAvennie and Tony Cottee.

Manager John Lyall had magnificently moulded a terrific team and the side didn't change much throughout the course of the season which obviously helped.

Five players had come through the famous West Ham Academy – Martin, Dickens, Parris, Pike and Cottee.

Three players had come down from Scotland – McAvennie from St Mirren, Stewart from Dundee United and Orr from Morton. Goalkeeping legend Parkes came from QPR, Gale from Fulham, Walford from Norwich and Ward from Oldham.

There was also a £5,000 signing from non-league Southall who turned into a bit of a bargain.

His name was Alan Devonshire or, as we just used to call him, Alan Dev. What a player. He was not far behind Billy Bonds on my shortlist of childhood heroes.

A couple of years ago I met Alan, surprisingly for the first time since his playing days, when he was manager of Braintree Town. As he spoke to me I'm pretty sure I came across like the nervous but excited schoolboy I was when I first saw him play.

I'm not sure if Alan twigged as much but I was definitely a bit starstruck, even though he's just an ordinary straightforward bloke. Well, never ordinary as far as I'm concerned! It's good that there are people around who can still have that kind of effect on you I guess, even in your late 40s. Or was I just being a big wuss? Okay, I know the answer to that really.

Luckily I later got to work in the media with Alvin Martin, Tony Gale and Tony Cottee. I've seen a fair bit of Steve Walford too as he is usually to be found on Martin O'Neill's coaching staff and usually searching for a nook or cranny in a football stadium to have a crafty fag!

In that breathtaking season McAvennie and Cottee scored an astonishing 54 goals between them, 28 for Frank, 26 for Tony. Only Gary Lineker scored more goals than McAvennie in the First

Division as it was called then. Whatever happened to him?!

The boys of 86 done well. So very well. Great players and great blokes. Thirty years on they have remained very close, and how very close they came to winning the league title for West Ham United.

I missed one game that season and guess which one? Guess which bloody one?

The date was 21 April 1986.

The game was West Ham 8 (EIGHT) Newcastle 1.

I'd started a new job at BBC Television Centre that day and couldn't get across London in time for the game. Alvin Martin scored a hat-trick against three (YES, THREE!) different goalkeepers and one of them was Peter Beardsley. Peter bloody Beardsley! I've still not forgiven Alvin for doing that in my absence but hey, give me time, I might one day. These are the games of our lives. Except I wasn't even there. Bloody typical.

'The Good Year' for West Ham became a rather decent year for me personally too. At the end of that most memorable of seasons I won a competition on Essex Radio to become the new stadium announcer at Upton Park, seeing off 150 other applicants. A dream job if ever there was one.

I actually lived in north London at the time, ironically near Arsenal's old stadium at Highbury, so the Essex Radio signal wasn't the best. The contenders had been whittled down to two and we both worked for the BBC funnily enough. I had a very crackly reception on the radio as I listened that summer Saturday afternoon. I wasn't even sure I had won. I had and started for the following season, 1986/87.

The players had a tough act to follow after finishing third the season before. I had a tough act to follow too because my predecessor on the tannoy, a smashing fellow called Bill Remfry, had been there for a quarter of a century. West Ham were that kind of club when it came to employing people although I wouldn't last anywhere near as long as Bill.

There were no giant screens or hi-tech speakers back then and I'm not sure much of what I announced could be clearly heard over the rather ancient public address system at Upton Park. I was still using an old-fashioned record player and it sometimes slowed down for no particular reason, ruining many a tune. I didn't care much, I was busy having the time of my life working for the team of my dreams.

That record player always seemed to be at the correct speed whenever I played the Hammers' famous theme song 'I'm Forever Blowing Bubbles' as the teams emerged from the tunnel on to the field of play. That tune used to make the hairs on the back of my neck stand up. It still does!

I even went to youth and reserve matches to announce the scorers to a couple of hundred people, mostly friends and family of the players! Billy Bonds, him again, was then in charge of the youth team and prior to one FA Youth Cup tie there was some confusion over who was wearing what shirt numbers which back then were 1-11. Those were the days!

Billy wasn't overly keen on paperwork so handed me the official teamsheet and told me to fill the names and numbers in. Little things please little minds and that certainly pleased mine. It's not every day you get to assist your childhood hero.

A lovely lady called Edna Sheridan used to run the office side of things at the Boleyn Ground and I still exchange Christmas cards with her to this day. A lot of brilliant people who worked there when I did were still working there when I returned to commentate at the stadium. Special people at a special club.

John Lyall was the manager and one of my jobs was to get the teamsheet off him an hour or so before kick-off so I could pass the line-ups on to fans over the tannoy. I was more than a little nervous about this task when I first started because I thought I might be rather in awe of a man who had been a big part of my childhood without even knowing it.

I needn't have worried. John used to invite me into his office for a cuppa, a sandwich and a chat before passing on the relevant information. There would often be famous footballing figures in his office or the opposing manager was present. John would always introduce them to me. Priceless moments.

When John Lyall was sacked by West Ham I wrote him a letter thanking him for everything he had done for me and for making me feel so welcome. Naturally he replied. It was a standard letter saying how overwhelmed he had been at the response of supporters and the kind sentiments expressed. At the bottom of the letter he'd handwritten, 'Sorry it's not personally written Ian but as you can imagine I have had literally hundreds to reply to. My thanks for all your help. JL'

That was personal enough for me. That letter remains a prized possession of mine. He was a very special manager but also a very special man.

In April 2006, John Lyall died of a heart attack at the age of just 66. I shed a few tears that day.

When I started as the man on the mic at Upton Park *EastEnders* had just started on the BBC and some of the cast were big West Ham fans who became regulars in the hospitality suite at Upton Park. I remember bumping into Nick Berry and Leslie Grantham quite a bit and I was working for the BBC at the time so I always lobbed that fact in to try and get them talking. Not that they were particularly interested in the reams of boring contracts I was churning out in front of the Television Locations Unit's green flickering word processor.

Leslie played one of the soap's top characters, Dirty Den, and he was big news at the time. He seemed a decent bloke who was a little surprised at the level of interest the tabloids were taking in his life.

He said he was pulling out in his car one day when a newspaper photographer suddenly jumped out in front of him from nowhere to take a snap. Leslie braked quickly to avoid him and then got out to check he was all right. Sure enough the story splashed on the front page next day was 'Dirty Den tried to run me over'. That's showbiz!

West Ham have always had lots of celebrity fans and these days there are the likes of Russell Brand, James Corden and Ray Winstone. Strangely, in somewhat of a design fault, you have to cut through Ray Winstone's executive box to reach the lower gantry at Upton Park these days.

I was working with Tony Gale one day but he'd been delayed going to the gantry and I was in a rush to get there. So off I trundled past Ray and his pals as they tucked into their lunch only for him to bark, 'Who the hell are you?' in a manner that actually quite scared me, as indeed did some of the hard men characters he portrayed!

Ray knew Tony well but not me so I could see his point as an intruder swept by. I name-dropped Tony and all was fine. He even offered me some wine. That might've made for an interesting commentary but I resisted!

It's hard to distinguish between fact and fiction when you see a list of famous West Ham fans that includes Barack Obama, Matt Damon, John Cleese and Keira Knightly. I read somewhere that even Alfred Hitchcock was a Hammer. Well, he would certainly have enjoyed the suspense.

I used to write a column in the club's matchday programme and in their monthly newspaper *Hammers News*. Having initially wanted to work in newspapers I loved writing and was in my element contributing in that way, although I was probably writing a load of old nonsense!

I received letters galore from the fans and used to read out birthday, wedding and anniversary dedications over the tannoy. I was loving it. When I said it was my dream job I wasn't kidding. Although I somehow managed to get into a bit of bother once.

The date was 6 October 1987.

It was all so very bloody West Ham. After a goalless draw in the first leg of a League Cup clash with Barnsley we were 2-0 up and cruising in the second leg. From nowhere Barnsley made it 2-2 and proceeded to absolutely wallop us 5-2 in extra time. As the fans filed out miserably at the end I announced something like, 'Tonight's attendance is 15,372 and we'll be lucky to get the 372 on Saturday after that.'

It raised a titter from the fans at the time but someone from the Football League heard it and was distinctly unimpressed. The governing body issued instructions to all 92 clubs to ensure their PA announcers were professional at all times.

It didn't mention what had prompted that message so West Ham's steely commercial manager Brian Blower got on the blower and rang the League for some gossip as to which club announcer had been so naughty, only to be told it was his own. Ooops!

In the starkest of contrast I made an announcement that included the most emotional, powerful, heart-wrenching words I've ever uttered anywhere and ever will. West Ham had just lost 2-1 at home to Southampton and were in relegation bother. At the full-time whistle the fans were restless and it threatened to turn a little nasty.

But the date was 15 April 1989.

I announced the details of the ongoing horror of Hillsborough and the initial death toll. My voice was shaking. The whole ground fell absolutely silent in a second.

The PA box I worked from was in the corner of the ground overlooking the visiting fans. I remember seeing the shock on their faces as my words came out. One looked up with arms outstretched mouthing 'what?' and 'no, no'.

We were all dazed by the early reality of such an immense tragedy and the immediate feeling that it could have been any one of us. I say reality although at the time, in the immediate aftermath, I'm not sure anyone could actually comprehend it as real. I found myself slowly repeating the details because I couldn't really believe what I was saying.

It's still hard to fathom the enormity of events that day. As it is to fathom why it took so long to find justice for the 96. Whenever I go to Anfield

now I always pause by the Hillsborough Memorial.
I think everyone should. It's the very least we can
do. You'll Never Walk Alone.

4

I Dreamed a Dream

MY West Ham gig meant working on matchdays only. I was hardly going to head to Upton Park and talk over the tannoy to an empty stadium at 9am on Friday morning. Although such was my affection for the club and my love of the job that, come to think of it, I wouldn't have put that past me.

My main employment at the time was at the BBC in its Television Locations Unit at White City, near Shepherd's Bush in west London. I basically sat in front of a word processor typing up legal contracts to cover the many and varied places where the BBC filmed.

Word processors were in their early days with green screens that flickered to bits. No wonder I ended up wearing specs when staring at them all day. They definitely did my eyes in! I also worked as a studio usher on a variety of comedy shows, showing audiences to their seats for *Only Fools and Horses*, *In Sickness and in Health*, *Wogan*, *Bread*, *'Allo 'Allo*, Les Dawson's *Blankety Blank*, *Bob's Full House* and many more.

We were supposed to keep an eye on the audience during the recording of these shows. Sorry health and safety busybodies but I was too busy watching the shows, the audience can bloody well look after themselves.

My personal favourites were probably predictable. Del Boy, Rodney and Uncle Albert. David Jason, Nicholas Lyndhurst and Buster Merryfield.

There was one recording where they had to keep re-doing one scene over 20 times because they couldn't stop laughing at John Sullivan's magnificent script. Not just a mild grin either, they were virtually rolling about on the floor. When that scene actually went out on television there was still a big smirk on their faces but I presume that was the only acceptable usable 'take'. Pure comedy gold. There may never be show another like it.

I was also a big fan of Bob Monkhouse. He warmed up his own audience to get them in the mood and it didn't take long. 'Everyone laughed when I said I wanted to be a comedian. Well, hey, they're not laughing now' used to have me chortling loudly every single time he told it and no matter that I heard it every week. It still makes me laugh now.

Likewise, 'I want to die like my father, peacefully in his sleep, not screaming or terrified like his passengers.'

Bob's TV career involved mainly family orientated shows but his live act was much more near the knuckle. He would use some of his naughtier lines in the warm-up in front of coach-loads of OAPs on a day trip to Television Centre. The look on their faces was a picture. They loved it. Bob Monkhouse was a genius.

Warren Mitchell similarly used to stir the audience himself before filming *In Sickness and in Health*. I saw him go close to offending people a few times. He was about as edgy as they come but played Alf Garnett to perfection.

Alf was a magnificent creation by another brilliant writer in Johnny Speight and of course Alf was a big West Ham fan, although Warren himself favoured Spurs in real life. The things you have to do as an actor. Wear a West Ham scarf as a Spurs fan. Ouch.

In Sickness and in Health was a comedy for its day and what struck me most was that the black members of the audience used to laugh the loudest. I can't imagine a modern day version would last too long though. The politically correct brigade would have a field day.

Terry Wogan used to film his thrice-weekly live chat show at a theatre down the road from Television Centre in Shepherd's Bush. For one such show a coach-load due to be in the audience had been stuck in London traffic. There's a shock. Some BBC staff were asked to fill their seats so it didn't look like the theatre was half empty.

Off I trotted to the Dress Circle and sat in the front row to get a great view. Little did I realise that this was the night Wogan began his show perched at the front of the Dress Circle asking questions of some of the audience. What? He never bloody starts the show sat up there, why today of all days?

I was sat right next to him absolutely dreading he might ask me something. I wasn't ready for a TV debut thank you very much. I doubt if Wogan even realised BBC staff were making up his audience numbers but he must have seen the frightened look on my face because he chose to chat to the person next to me. I decided if I ever had to sit in the audience again the back row would do for me.

Les Dawson was another who used to have me in tears and the great thing with Les was that he didn't have to do much. He just had that kind of face didn't he? He would walk on the stage and everyone would laugh before he'd even said anything. Another genius taken from us too soon.

I used to imagine what it would've been like to watch *Morecambe and Wise*, *The Two Ronnies*, *Porridge* and *Fawlty Towers* being recorded. Sadly they were before my time as a BBC usher. Even so, it was an immense privilege to see so many class comedians and actors at such close quarters. And comedy shows were definitely funnier back then!

I eventually landed a production job behind the scenes at BBC Radio 2, working with the likes of Ken Bruce, Gloria Hunniford, John Dunn and former Fleet Street newspaper editor Derek Jameson, who was certainly a character.

When I first worked on his breakfast show he asked me to come through to the studio with a bowl of cornflakes and some milk during the 8am news bulletin. It was a long bulletin which allowed him time to consume his breakfast.

As I returned to the gallery the technical boys were cowering and Derek had a face like thunder. It was explained to me that he liked his milk already poured on to his flakes rather than having to do it himself. Sod that! Needless to say whenever I took him breakfast again I always left the milk for him to do. I'd make a useless waiter.

Derek wasn't as precious as I've just made him sound in fairness. I enjoyed working on his show and his lively newspaper past interested me as that was the career path I had initially wanted to go down.

Derek certainly generated a lively response to his radio show. One of my jobs was to sift through the many letters he received from listeners. Some of those letters absolutely slaughtered him. They were horrible letters from horrible people. One got through to him by accident one day and he was really upset by the vitriol.

I vowed that if I was ever in a position where I received such venom I would laugh it off and not let it get to me. That vow has served me well on Twitter after a big game when some general abuse would head my way over something I said or quite often, something I didn't actually say because it's surprising how many folk mishear you. I don't think there's a swear word I've not seen. Whatever, bring it on.

I really enjoyed working with Gloria Hunniford although I didn't really 'produce' her as such. Gloria had been at the top of her game for years. There wasn't much she didn't know and she hardly needed a young whippersnapper like me issuing instructions. I just hovered in the control gallery next to her studio and let her get on with it. I happily sat back watching another top broadcaster do their stuff. I listened and learned.

Gloria used to have many celebrity guests on her show and I used to go and collect them from reception. Of the many big names I ushered to the studio the one I remember most funnily enough is Captain Mark Phillips. I expected Princess Anne's then husband to be quite a serious man and obviously a tad posh. Yet he chatted merrily away all the way to the studio asking lots of questions about me and my job. Another who seemed genuinely interested in other people. Good on yer Captain!

I made my debut on professional radio during the BBC's annual Children in Need fundraiser. Producer Carolyn Smyth kindly let me go on-air during Scottish presenter Ken Bruce's show, which I worked on at the time. There has always been a Scot around when something happens in my career and it was Ken for starters.

It was only for a couple of minutes and I was a nervous wreck, certainly compared to the dulcet tones of Mr Bruce, but it left me wanting more. Ken remains on Radio 2 to this day and no wonder, he's a top professional but also a top person.

West Ham were playing Nottingham Forest that week and I offered to donate £5 per goal scored in the game to Children in Need. That sounds a bit mean now but it must've been quite a lot back then! Typically there were five goals in the first half alone! It finished 3-3, well it was never going to be 0-0 was it.

I had my picture taken with Hammers striker Leroy Rosenior and it made the local paper. I would get to work with Leroy years later too in this tiny little world we live in. And then I would get to commentate on his son Liam, naturally!

Although I had been applying for jobs in BBC Sport I really enjoyed working at Radio 2. I landed a trainee producer attachment and came up with loads of ideas for programmes. The problem being there were so many producers back in those days that my ideas went from the controller's in-tray to out-tray pretty quickly. In fact I should have just put them in the out-tray to save time.

I was a big fan of the new musicals of the time, *Les Miserables* and *Phantom of the Opera*. They were new in the mid-1980s but they're still going strong, very strong. I could happily listen to the complete symphonic version of *Les Miserables* all day long. The recent film soundtrack isn't bad either but then I'm a sucker for pretty much any version of that fantastic musical. I've even listened to foreign language versions. Yes I'm hooked to that extent, a total *Les Mis* saddo!

I've seen *Les Miserables* 20 times and *Phantom of the Opera* 16 times. If I wasn't a football commentator I'd love to be performing as Jean Valjean or Inspector Javert or the Phantom himself. Admittedly I would need a few million singing and acting lessons first so it remains a dream I dream.

Quite often while waiting to commentate on a gantry I sing myself songs from *Les Mis* to pump me up. I guess it's a bit like players listening to their music on their headphones or when you hear loud tunes blaring out of a dressing room pre-match. Although I don't think players ever have 'Bring Him Home' or 'Do You Hear The People Sing?' or my favourite song 'Stars' on their playlist. No, don't think so somehow.

I'd come up with a couple of ideas for Radio 2 programmes including 'Boublil and Schonberg: Masters of the House', telling the story of the creators of *Les Miserables* and how the musical came about and how it was panned by critics in the early days. 'Master of the House' is one of the best songs from the show.

Another of my programme ideas was 'Michael Crawford – Behind the Mask', telling the incredible life story of the man who once upon a time was brilliantly playing Frank Spencer in the BBC sitcom classic *Some Mothers Do 'Ave 'Em* and was then absolutely sensational as the Phantom. By the way he was pretty decent in *Barnum* too.

I had mapped out every single second of these shows in my mind. I was serious. Very. I'd even sorted out competition prizes for tickets to see the musicals in the West End and stay in a top hotel. I had gone a long way down the road in trying to get West End star Michael Ball and HRH Prince Edward to present these shows. Edward was working for Andrew Lloyd Webber's Really Useful Company so it seemed like a good idea at the time.

I'd already envisaged in my mind a picture of him on the front cover of *Radio Times* but I was getting a bit ahead of myself. I suddenly received a major rollocking for approaching Buckingham Palace with an initial inquiry. Apparently there's only one person at the BBC who was allowed to contact the royals and it sure as hell wasn't me! It was a member of the very senior management. Ooops!

Alas both my ideas were rejected as I was only a trainee producer and they were overstaffed with proper producers, fully trained ones! They had over 40 of those although I remember one guy who used to turn up in the office at 10am and was gone by midday, never to be seen again. He took long lunches to the extreme and further. The BBC was a bit like that then. You wouldn't get away with that in this day and age, you would hope!

I've kept a memo from my Radio 2 boss at the time telling me they weren't going to accept any Ian Crocker productions and didn't want any more Ian Crocker ideas so could I please stop sending them. Well, cheers for the bloody encouragement. Thanks a bundle.

Naturally, I ignored him and carried on sending ideas galore. I thoroughly researched a proposed Christmas special on an anniversary of the charts. It was all about the number one songs over the years but also those that didn't make it. You'd be surprised at some of the songs that never did.

The head of programmes probably set light to my proposal on its way to the bin but at Christmas a similar programme popped up in the schedules, with a senior producer in charge of it. Shame I didn't copyright the idea or take out a patent on it.

I wouldn't say I never took no for an answer because the answer was always no so I kind of had to, but it never stopped me trying. I've never been one for giving up on my dreams too easily. However I did become rather disillusioned that my programme ideas were never going to see the light of day. To quote another song from *Les Mis* I was definitely 'On My Own'.

I've kept those programme proposals (yes I know that's a bit sad) and I was looking back at them in preparation for this chapter. I still think they were bloody brilliant ideas but I accept I may be a bit biased in that respect. You've got to believe in yourself because I doubt other people will if you don't. Although in this instance, they didn't believe in me anyway.

While working at West Ham I bumped into Jonathan Pearce who had started a certain style of commentary on Capital Radio in London and he was very good at it. I was offered a weekend stint helping out in the studio and reading the sporting headlines and classified football results on air. I had to relinquish the tannoy at West Ham which was hard to take but I knew it was for the right reasons.

I've been broadcasting for a good while now but one of the best jobs I've ever had was reading the classifieds! You just felt that everyone was hanging on your every score. I was no James Alexander Gordon for sure. He was the master on BBC radio but I bloody loved doing those results! It just about made up for me badly missing the Upton Park tannoy.

I only worked for the BBC in office hours Monday to Friday so the personnel department was initially happy with me doing Capital shifts at weekends. I was surprised to be allowed though.

I had actually applied for many different sport jobs within the BBC's radio empire but failed miserably to land one. At one such interview, or 'board' as the BBC preferred to call them, I had thoroughly researched anything and everything to do with every sport in the world.

I wanted to cover all bases in case they asked me a series of questions. Yet the only sport-related question they asked turned out to be about the Gleneagles Agreement and its importance in world sport. What?! I could've told them who the reigning tiddlywinks world champion was and they ask about the bloody Gleneagles Agreement. A BBC 'board' could be like that. Little wonder that 'bored' is pronounced the same way.

It narked me that under broadcasting jobs in the staff magazine *Ariel* it would say, 'Essential: University degree. Desirable: Good broadcasting voice.' I felt that should be the other way round. Mainly because I didn't have a university degree!

I believed the BBC should have given its existing staff a chance to do some of these jobs, to promote from within. As you can probably gather I didn't so much have a bee in my bonnet, it was a full blown hive.

I wrote to the editor of *Ariel* about it, and the head of personnel, and the head of local radio. Oh, and the director general, Michael Checkland. Oh, and the chairman of the BBC at the time, Stuart Young. Before you ask yes I have been sad enough to keep all the letters and looking back through them I can't believe how many people I pestered. I was only in my 20s but I must have come across as a young Victor Meldrew.

My protests prompted quite a debate on the letters page of *Ariel* and the chairman sent me a three-page reply – he obviously had too much time on his hands! The director general kept it short but succinct:

'I have every sympathy with the problems you have encountered in widening your BBC experience and I very much hope that you were not given unrealistic promises when you decided to join the BBC. I have passed your letter to the new Managing Director of Regional Broadcasting.

'In the meantime I continue to support Birmingham City – we all have our problems!'

A few years later I would get to appreciate that last point from Michael Checkland!

I don't think for one minute anyone had given me unrealistic promises, but there's a chance I might have pretended they had! Not that any sympathy vote was likely to be forthcoming.

I plugged away but knew it was a losing battle when a BBC radio chief told me I had a Cockney accent anyway which was never going to work on radio as it was deemed 'unsuitable'. These days accents are very much IN but back then they were definitely OUT. Especially at the BBC.

Not that I felt I actually had any particular accent although maybe living in London and going to West Ham a lot had an effect on my vocal chords. Maybe it was a strange mix of a Dorset country accent with a strong hint of Cockney. Either way, I couldn't Adam or Eve it.

The BBC's personnel department soon had me by the Niagaras. After a year or so of working weekends and midweek evenings at Capital I was suddenly summoned to a fearsome personnel lady called Marjolyn (even the name seemed a bit scary).

I always used to think of Clint Eastwood's line from the *Dirty Harry* movie when he got transferred to personnel as a punishment, 'Personnel? That's for arseholes.'

I was itching to repeat Clint's fine words when Marjolyn angrily informed me I had been heard broadcasting on Capital Radio and wondered who on earth had given me permission to do that as a member of BBC staff. Er, the BBC's personnel actually. They then told me that had been a mistake on their part and I was ordered to give up the Capital work or resign from the BBC.

Nowadays personnel has been re-invented as human resources and I know a few folk who work in that so of course they're not arseholes anymore. That was only when they were called personnel!

I relayed Marjolyn's order to Jonathan Pearce. His boss at Capital was Richard Park, later to find fame in the BBC talent show *Fame Academy*. Although he was pretty famous in the radio industry by then having made his name in Glasgow with Radio Clyde. Another Scot who would have a big say in my career!

Richard could be quite fearsome as well but he and Jonathan offered me a permanent job at Capital Radio. From an early age I'd dreamt of working for the BBC but it was time to say goodbye, much earlier than I thought I might have.

It was soon time to say hello to my first commentary. That's what I liked about Jonathan, Richard and Capital. They just threw you in the deep end, the best way to learn.

The date was 5 November 1991.

The game was Barnet 4 Carlisle 2. I shared the commentary with Steve Wilson, now heard on the BBC's *Match of the Day*. We were both making our debuts. I remember thinking he was rather better at it than me and I certainly remember thinking I was bloody awful.

Oh well, you've got to start somewhere. These are the games of our lives. Although I doubt in the history of football commentary anyone will particularly remember remember that fifth of November.

Apart from Steve and I.

5

Capital Gains

AS well as Steve Wilson the sports team at Capital Radio included Julian Walters, Rob Wotton and Dave Clark who all went on to work for Sky Sports. And of course Jonathan Pearce who later worked for Sky Sports too, Five, and the BBC. Like Steve he is now a frontrunner on *Match of the Day*.

A reporter called Andy Edwards guided me into the job and he knew everything about everything to do with sport and radio. He was a huge help to me.

There was also a top producer called Pete Simmons who held it, and me, together a few times. A young lad called Darren King helped out on the production side too and is now a director on Sky Sports News. Jim Proudfoot was there too, now on talkSPORT. It's a small world. The boys done well, all of them.

As proved with Barnet v Carlisle, Capital were quite happy to throw you in at the deep end. Nobody was asking for a university degree thank goodness. Phew! I had always hoped for a long career in the BBC but at the time they would never take such a chance on you. I learnt so much so quickly at Capital although I had been doing hospital radio for many years and that had given me an excellent grounding in all things radio.

I had presented a few sports shows and spun a few discs as a DJ on Radio Moorfields at the world famous Moorfields Eye Hospital in the City of London. The station was run, and had been for years, by a guy called Ivor Gilbert who was a brilliant character, sadly no longer with us but probably still trying to broadcast up above. I owe him.

We used to go round the wards asking for requests and I must've played Stevie Wonder's 'I Just Called to Say I Love You' and Chris De Burgh's 'Lady in Red' a billion times.

Being an eye hospital there was a very good chance the patients would leave the building one day. Unlike in ordinary hospitals where Frank Sinatra's 'My Way' was banned from the list of patient requests despite its considerable popularity.

The reason made sense. 'And now the end is near…
and I must face the final curtain.'

We did it our way at Radio Moorfields and we
had an absolute blast. I recorded interviews with
the likes of film buff Barry Norman, magician
Paul Daniels, quiz show host Steve Jones and the
Phantom of the Opera of the day, Dave Willetts.
Dave was a top man and the interview took place
in his dressing room at the theatre just before he
was fitted with the Phantom's mask and make-up.
Any excuse for me to go behind the scenes in a West
End theatre!

Years later I was having a bite to eat at Oxford
Services and who should be on the next table but
Paul Daniels and Debbie McGee. I was itching
to remind Paul of the interview I did for Radio
Moorfields even though I knew he probably
wouldn't remember it at all. I didn't really want
to interrupt them though but then the waitress
delivered my garlic bread to their table by mistake.
And they were going to eat it the cheeky pair! I
couldn't resist a 'blimey you nearly made my garlic
bread disappear there…now that's magic'. Debbie
laughed. Bless her. Paul didn't even come close. I
didn't bother with the Moorfields reminiscing.

Hospital radio was a terrific breeding ground
for so many radio enthusiasts. There were guys

on the station who should've gone on to broadcast professionally. My old mate Hugh Vale for one had a terrific voice. He stuck with a career in the Civil Service but recently started doing some radio after taking early retirement. I'm glad he got there in the end.

I had the radio bug for sure. Over the years I had written to every radio station in the UK looking for a job whether in front of the microphone or behind the scenes or making the tea. It is actually genuinely surprising how many tea-makers at radio stations went on to greater things. It really did happen and I hope it still does.

Although it worked for many no professional station actually fancied my tea-making abilities. I've kept all the replies and read through them again just the other day to remind me what a load of tosh 'we'll keep your details on file' is. Lies, damned lies!

During my time at the BBC I had visited many of its local radio stations touting for work. They were very good at letting you look around the studios in fairness, but less forthcoming in actually giving you a job.

I was a regular at BBC Radio Kent and BBC Radio Bedfordshire who were so very accommodating I felt like I did work there at times. A guy called Jim Latham ended up as programme director at both stations and was always forthcoming with advice, considering he must have thought I was stalking him, which come to think of it I probably was.

I sent Jim demo tapes regularly and he replied with a hand-written letter to one saying, 'When you pick up the script you've got to sound more natural. The join between off-the-cuff chat and script reading should be seamless. You also rushed reading the news and could afford to slow the pace. I'd suggest a lot more work on the voice. Your "th" sounds are coming out as "f" but not all the time, just enough to be irritating. Sorry about the acid, it's late on Saturday night.'

The acid was welcome. I wanted constructive criticism and Jim was one of the few to provide it. By the way I think I still do that 'th' and 'f' thing now. So much for taking his advice on board. Jim took the time to offer help and I always remember him whenever anyone now asks me for advice on how to become a football commentator. I'm not sure if my advice is any good but at least I always reply! Just as Jim always did.

I also visited a few commercial radio stations and was a big fan of LBC in London. I used to love its breakfast show in particular, hosted by consummate professionals Douglas Cameron and Bob Holness. I dropped them a letter about something and they read it out on air. I was well chuffed! Bob later did a fabulous job on the TV quiz *Blockbusters*, especially when students asked him for a 'P'.

Steve Allen, who hosted the night-time shows, was particularly welcoming, so much so that I ended up in an interesting gentlemen's club after one of his shows. That was an eye-opener for this country bumpkin!

I also watched LBC's Saturday afternoon sports show go out live one day. It was hosted by a guy called Jeff Stelling. Whatever happened to him?

So after years of trying, after all the letters and all the rejections, here I was at Capital Radio, London. Having pestered local radio stations from Inverness to Exeter, from Aberdeen to Brighton to here to there to everywhere I'd landed a job bang in the middle of England's capital city on the Euston Road.

I soon found myself reading breakfast bulletins on Tony Blackburn's show, then bumping into broadcasting legends at every corridor turn such as Kenny Everett, Mike Read, David Hamilton, Paul Burnett and Chris Tarrant.

Kenny was a fascinating character and was present for possibly one of my least successful commentaries. I was given the sizeable task of commentating on The Derby. Not from Epsom but sat in the studio opposite Kenny watching the live television pictures. 'Off-tube' as they say in the business.

I was rather nervous to say the least as horse racing isn't a strong point for me and all the different jockey colours seemed rather confusing. To this day I am full of admiration for horse racing commentators. The only other non-football commentary I've ever done was on a swimming tournament and hands up, I was bloody hopeless at that too.

I didn't know Kenny that well as we never normally did sport bulletins on his show. Although you would see him around the Capital studios and he certainly had a considerable presence. He was the sort of guy you soon felt like you'd known for ages.

He could sense that I was on the brink of crapping myself ahead of my horse racing commentating debut and quickly put me at ease, mostly by being very funny, which he was rather good at. He certainly helped me that day.

Kenny was only 50 when he died. If he was still going now I rather suspect he'd still be on the radio having a right old hoot and probably upsetting a few folk along the way. Good on him.

I used to watch Mike Read on *Saturday Superstore* on BBC1 of a Saturday morning. Now

I was reading bulletins on his weekday drive-time show. The hours were long in the sport department at Capital, and I mean very long, but that was the nature of the job. Nobody complained. We knew it was the job to have.

Once, after a particularly exhausting schedule without much downtime at all, my throat started to go very dry when reading bulletins and I'd be seriously worried that I wasn't going to get through them. I'd never experienced anything like that before.

Mike calmed me down and said if I seized up and couldn't actually speak he'd take over and make a laugh out of it. I managed to struggle through the bulletins despite the self-doubt but he was such a calming influence. He suggested I needed a holiday to rest and recuperate. A holiday later I was fine and never had such problems again. It's a funny old game.

David 'Diddy' Hamilton was a great guy with a magnificent broadcasting voice and he later became matchday tannoy announcer at his beloved Fulham. Last time I looked he was still there and sounds rather better than that fella who used to do the same at West Ham all those years ago.

Chris Tarrant's breakfast show on Capital FM was brilliant. Sometimes my shift would start at

6.30am, the same time as his show, yet he'd be rushing through reception at 6.29am. Not a man to waste time and a complete natural on the radio. And on television come to that.

I had to read some Cricket World Cup bulletins on his show once and as he handed over to me he lit up a big cigar. As a mild asthma sufferer that was definitely the wheeziest broadcast I've ever done. Tarrant just chuckled away in the background.

On the football front at Capital I got to work with Bobby Moore, England's World Cup-winning captain. Like I needed to remind anyone. Although actually sometimes it was worth reminding him.

Bobby was a fantastic man. He would ring up the office and spend ten minutes asking you about yourself. That's what he was like. It was never about him when perhaps it should've been. He never really struck you as the man who had lifted the Jules Rimet Trophy for England.

I did a game at West Bromwich Albion with him and he drove us to the West Midlands from London. They were playing his team, and mine, West Ham. He dropped me off at the media entrance at The Hawthorns before going off to park. I asked for Capital Radio's passes at the reception and the guy said, in all seriousness and not realising his error, 'Which one are you? Bobby Moore?' If only.

As you can imagine Bobby had a stack of stories to tell but one of my favourites actually concerned a youth cup game he played in at Old Trafford which went the distance. Bobby couldn't work out why West Ham were getting swamped at the start of the second period of extra time. They'd been pretty comfortable in the first period.

Then it dawned on him. They only had ten men, or boys, on the pitch. One of the lads had gone to the toilet without realising the turnaround was immediate at half-time in extra time. He went for the full works too, not just a wee. I know it doesn't sound like his funniest ever story and it wasn't but it was just the way Bobby told it. He had me rolling around the passenger seat. Just as well he was driving. Priceless.

I was working at Capital on the day of Bobby's tragic death from cancer in 1993 and on the morning after I had to read news bulletins on Tony Blackburn's breakfast show. Bobby's death was dominating those bulletins.

I was close to choking to be honest and it didn't help that Tony felt I was overdoing the story and said he was going to complain to management. As I left his studio he was muttering, 'He's only a footballer after all,' which rather missed the point. Because he wasn't only a footballer. Not at all.

He did complain and management ticked him off rather than me which he didn't take too well. Our boss gave it, 'I employ lots of different people for lots of different reasons and where Tony is concerned having a f***ing brain isn't one of them.'

We knew that was rather harsh, and actually unfair and untrue, but it lightened the mood at the time and gave everyone a laugh for the first time in a while as we mourned the loss of a great man in Bobby Moore.

Bobby had endeared himself to all of us and I have no idea how I kept it together during those bulletins, or when I covered the games after his death when West Ham played at Sunderland and then home to Wolves, amid tributes galore of course. These days I blubber at *Long Lost Family* and *DIY SOS*. Bobby would've been embarrassed at anyone blubbering for him so maybe that was why I pulled it off.

Tony Blackburn's remarkable career speaks for itself and it's hard to envisage a time when he won't be on the radio. He used to tell me a joke off air every morning just before he told it on air, almost like he was looking to see what my reaction would be. Although I somehow doubt my reaction would have stopped him telling it anyway. He always looked pretty proud of those gags.

They were along the lines of, 'What's red and lies upside down in the gutter?' The answer was a dead London bus. Of course! You might not consider it funny and you might be right but on those early morning shifts I always looked forward to those jokes. They made me laugh anyway.

Tony was a funny man although he did flummox me on air one morning when I reported on some football hooliganism which was prevalent at the time. At the end of the bulletin he piped up, 'Tell me Ian, why do these fans cause trouble?' Tricky question to answer that. Tony didn't like football and it showed. I'm not sure how I did answer that question but suspect I talked utter tripe! Not for the first time, or indeed the last.

After the disagreement over Bobby Moore I never worked on Tony's breakfast show again but can't say I was overly bothered. It meant not having to get up at 4am. I prefer the other end of the day. Not nightclubs, evening kick-offs. I really missed those rubbish jokes though!

Jonathan Pearce dominated the Capital commentaries and it was hard to argue with that. Steve Wilson and Julian Waters backed him up and were ahead of me in the commentary queue. Julian is now a presenter on Sky Sports News and doesn't commentate any more which is a shame

CAPITAL GAINS

because he was very good at it during those radio days.

The Capital Radio Group had taken over the iconic station BRMB in England's second city, Birmingham. I was offered a transfer from London (possibly of the Bosman variety) to be the number one commentator covering Aston Villa, Birmingham City, West Bromwich Albion, Wolverhampton Wanderers and Walsall.

I loved working at Capital because it didn't just cover football. I'd got to interview the likes of Linford Christie, Sally Gunnell, Damon Hill, Frank Bruno and Lennox Lewis and Capital also covered the All-England Tennis Championships at Wimbledon from a private commentary box on the Centre Court. As a tennis lover, that was sheer bliss, a fantastic fortnight. Bring on the strawberries and cream.

So there was a lot to consider about leaving London, the powerhouse of so many things, especially in the media. But I wanted to commentate on football more often and saw a world of opportunity ahead in that respect.

I'd always wanted a career in the BBC and had given that up a couple of years earlier. I'd always wanted to live and work in London and now I was about to give that up. I'd left Weymouth for

London at the age of just 17. I was a naïve country boy for sure.

I lived in a bedsit in Finsbury Park in north London, a solitary room which was barely bigger than a wardrobe of the non-walk-in variety. It wasn't the best of areas back then. The house was near the local red light district and on heading home late at night the ladies would offer a 'fancy any business love?' I'd find myself politely saying, 'No thanks, I'm okay,' in a very shy Dorset boy kind of way. What a total numpty I must have looked.

There was no washing machine in the house so I used the local launderette and on one visit some local nutter walked in, smashed a bottle and threatened me with the jagged edge. Jesus Christ, I was only trying to wash my pants! Fortunately a big bloke at the other end of the launderette raced up and launched himself at this nutter, taking him out completely. The police turned up and hauled the nutter away. That launderette was never the same for me after that near miss.

The big city had beckoned after I had failed to land a job on my local paper, the *Dorset Evening Echo*, which would have suited me fine and was my initial ambition in adult life. I still keep in touch with the *Echo*'s general manager at the time, Brian Makepeace. We exchange Christmas cards every year so I've got over that rejection! I often wonder how different life might have been had Brian actually given me a job.

My first job was actually cleaning caravans in the local holiday park, Waterside, at Bowleaze Cove. I specialised in Brillo-padding ovens but didn't quite fancy a career in it, even though I thought I was rather good at making those ovens spotless. I felt a sense of achievement seeing them gleaming.

In between Brillo-padding I produced my first batch of letters asking for a job and sent them to every TV station, radio station, newspaper, publisher and media company in the land. It worked, eventually, a few thousand Brillo pads later.

I was offered a job in the sales department at J. Whitaker and Sons Publishers in central London. It was renowned mainly for the information bible *Whitaker's Almanack* which had been going for many, many years. It included all sorts of statistics covering just about everything, most of which bored me to tears, but I left that opinion out of my sales pitch. The company also published the trade publication *The Bookseller*.

It was a terrific business to work for and gave me a start in life and in London. I was there for a few years before landing a job at the BBC. I will always be grateful to Sally and David Whitaker.

These are the kind of people who decide the course of your life.

So after 12 years in London would it really be right to give up everything I had worked so hard for in the Big Smoke? Or rather, everything I had pestered an awful lot of people for. I thought and thought and thought about the implications but I couldn't really think what would be for the best. My indecision was final. Then I split up with my girlfriend at the time. Decision made. That was the kick up the Brum I needed.

6

A Kick Up The Brum

ASTON Villa and Birmingham City. Ron Atkinson and Barry Fry. Dull moments were not so much rare, they were pretty much non-existent with those two great characters bossing England's second city in the early-to-mid-1990s.

I remember going to interview Big Ron for the first time at Villa's Bodymoor Heath Training Ground. I was sat in his big office along with the rather more experienced members of the Midlands hack pack, national newspaper journalists for whom the area had been their 'patch' for years.

Big Ron suggested the youngest person in the room should make the tea for everyone. That'll be me then. I trembled as I lifted a giant well-used silver teapot thinking I was almost certainly going to drop it all over Big Ron's desk and probably Big Ron himself.

I saw him edge back in his seat, probably expecting the same. I survived, he survived, and that was as nervous as it got with Ron. He was different class. I've never seen a teapot as large as that since but then that was Ron. Everything seemed big, even his name. And his teapot.

A couple of months later Villa were drawn to play the Spanish side Deportivo La Coruna in Europe. We stayed at the same hotel as Villa for the away leg and ended up poolside with Big Ron, his natural habitat methinks. A few of us participated in a quiz about anything and everything to do with football but there was no catching out Big Ron. His knowledge was immense, he knew all the answers.

He had some answers out on the pitch too, guiding Villa to League Cup glory in 1994. The first stop on their road to Wembley was close to home when they were drawn against city rivals Birmingham in a two-legged affair and beat them 1-0 on both occasions. It gave me my first taste of the Second City Derby and it remains one of my favourite derbies. It's proper nasty.

In the third round Villa won 4-1 at Sunderland with Dalian Atkinson scoring twice. Dalian was a player who could frustrate or delight in equal measure. There wasn't much middle ground but on his day he was a decent watch.

Atkinson the player and Atkinson the manager were starting to sense this could be their year in the League Cup, or the Coca-Cola Cup as it was called that season. Dalian scored for Ron again in a 1-0 win at Arsenal in round four. They were back in north London in the quarter-finals and won 2-1 at Tottenham with Earl Barrett scoring the decisive goal.

When you've won away at Sunderland, Arsenal and Spurs you might be thinking your name is on the cup. Villa were then paired with Tranmere Rovers from a division below in the semi-finals. Wembley surely beckoned for Villa but nobody had told Tranmere who were 3-0 up in the first leg at Prenton Park.

Crucially, Dalian Atkinson – yes, him again – snatched an injury-time reply for Villa that set up a second leg which, to this day, is probably the most dramatic match I've ever commentated on in England.

The date was 27 February 1994.

Villa stormed into a 2-0 lead to level the aggregate score with another Weymouth old boy, Shaun Teale, scoring the second goal (up the Terras!) but then John Aldridge planted a penalty after Mark Bosnich had brought him down.

Tranmere fans will tell you to this day that Bosnich should have been sent off for the challenge and they might have had a point. Bosnich stayed on and later became a pivotal figure.

With two minutes remaining Dalian Atkinson – yes, him again – made it 3-1 and forced extra time, during which Tranmere smacked the crossbar. It was the mother of all penalty shoot-outs. Villa and Tranmere both spurned what would've been winning spot-kicks by the time Bosnich saved from Ian Nolan to send Villa to Wembley.

It was an extraordinary night, right up with Old Firm games in terms of pure drama. After screaming my way through that epic contest for over two hours I couldn't speak for a week afterwards. My throat was in bits and ruins. Thankfully I recovered in time to commentate on my first Wembley final.

The date was 27 March 1994.

Villa beat Manchester United 3-1. Dean Saunders bagged two goals and Dalian Atkinson scored yet again which was evidently written in the League Cup stars. Captain Kevin Richardson lifted the trophy and I was delighted for him, a top pro and a top man.

It was such a sweet moment for Big Ron too, denying his former club a treble as it turned out. The final was also a great game but it never quite matched that breathtaking semi-final. Nothing much could, or has since for me. In England anyway!

The following season Europe beckoned again for Villa and so did another dramatic penalty shootout as Big Ron's side were drawn against UEFA Cup holders Inter Milan in the first round. That gave me a first taste of the San Siro and I've been fortunate enough to return to that iconic arena a few times since. It may be ageing but there's still something about it for sure.

Dennis Bergkamp scored the only goal of the first leg but a 1-0 defeat left Villa with a great chance in the return and Birmingham B6 was certainly buzzing that night.

The date was 29 September 1994.

Ray Houghton scored against Italian national goalkeeper Gianluca Pagliuca, as he had done at the World Cup a few months earlier. With the aggregate scores level, penalties loomed. We'd been here before.

It wasn't quite as crazy as the Tranmere shoot-out but it wasn't far off as Phil King stroked in the winning kick to send Villa through and to send Inter, Bergkamp and all, crashing out. It couldn't happen to a nicer guy than Kingy. What you saw was what you got from him.

In the second round Villa were drawn against the Turkish side Trabzonspor. The media flew out on the same plane as the team and we hit some horrible turbulence on the way over, possibly my worst experience of turbulence, although it's usually a bit choppy coming in to land in Scotland.

With all the newspaper, radio and TV reporters on board it became a big story. 'Villa players in near-miss drama'. Big Ron was asked for his opinion as reporters waited by the baggage belt in Trabzon, 'Yeah, it was so scary even the black players turned white.'

Everyone appreciated the humour, mostly the black players. Ron would later lose his job at ITV for highly offensive racist comments. They were utterly inexcusable but surprising too because I really don't think he was like that at all. You can only speak as you find.

Trabzonspor knocked out Villa so, despite that memorable night against Inter, the European campaign was short-lived in the days of straight knockout ties. Not long after that loss Big Ron was sacked by Villa chairman 'Deadly' Doug Ellis. He got through a few managers did Doug. I was sorry to see Big Ron go but typically he had given us some big memories.

Brian Little took over and Villa were back on the trail of the League Cup in 1996. The road to Wembley began with a 6-0 thumping of Peterborough and they then saw off Stockport 2-0 before beating QPR 1-0 to reach the quarter-finals.

Villa were drawn at home to West Midlands rivals Wolves and Tommy Johnson scored the only goal of the game. Arsenal awaited in the semi-finals. Dennis Bergkamp and Dwight Yorke traded doubles as the first leg ended 2-2. The second leg ended 0-0 which was enough to send Villa through to the final on the away goals rule. Here we go again. From Big to Little. Ron to Brian.

The date was 24 March 1996.

Villa comfortably beat a poor Leeds United side 3-0 to lift the League Cup once more. Serbian striker Savo Milosevic had been renamed 'Miss-a-lot-ovich' after a largely indifferent time in English football yet he scored a stunner in the final. 'Savo havo a Wembley goal,' I screamed. Kenneth Wolstenholme rest easy.

Local hero Ian Taylor and Dwight Yorke were fitting additions to the scoresheet in a one-sided affair. Villa had the FA Cup in their sights as well that season. They reached the semi-finals but lost to a Liverpool side who were lethal on the day, Robbie

Fowler in particular. Villa also finished fourth in the Premier League.

I really thought Little's Villa team would progress and enjoy further success and I said so on the radio. 'This could be the first of a few trophies.' Well, that was the kiss of death. I was wrong. I often am.

Within two years Little himself had departed. Ironically he had tried to sign Andy Cole to link up with Dwight Yorke at Villa. The two later linked up rather well at Manchester United. Football is littered with such tales of what might have been.

The likeable John Gregory took over as manager and did get Villa to an FA Cup Final, but they lost to Chelsea in 2000. I still keep in touch with John to this day. He's the only manager I've ever interviewed in a toilet. That occurred at Villa's training ground one day when it was a bit noisy with banter flying around so John locked the toilet door behind us for a bit of peace. I'm not sure I'll ever interview a manager in a toilet again. I'm not sure I want to.

In 1993 David Sullivan and the Gold brothers, David and Ralph, took over Birmingham City. They would later re-invigorate the Blues but nobody said it was going to be easy for starters. Karren Brady became chief executive and Barry Fry became manager. A mouth-watering combination for those of us in the media and sure enough there were stories, stories and then a few more stories.

With a dilapidated stadium, and that's being kind to it, Birmingham City Football Club looked on its last legs before Sullivan and Co. rode into town. In hindsight they were probably just what the club needed although a few months after their arrival Birmingham were relegated to the Second Division as it was then, actually the third tier of English football.

On arrival the ebullient Barry Fry had promised Blues fans he would get them out of the First Division and he did just that. Alas it was down to the Second! That was his joke by the way and he still tells it! Such is life when you are Birmingham City.

Their sorry demise however led to one of the most memorable of seasons; 1994/95 was one of the most enjoyable in a commentating career spanning a quarter of a century.

Either side of Villa reaching Wembley, Birmingham City only went and got there too in the Auto Windscreens Shield, the Football League Trophy which has had a few different sponsors over the years.

The road to Wembley started with a 5-3 win at Peterborough in which Jonathan Hunt scored a hat-trick. On a different day Hunt gave me my worst moment on radio but more on that later in this commentating journey.

Blues saw off Walsall, Gillingham and Hereford and then edged past Swansea City 3-2 after extra time. In the Southern Area Final they took a 1-0 lead into the second leg at Leyton Orient. Weymouth's finest, Steve Claridge, was in the mood, scoring twice in a 3-2 victory that meant the Blues were on their way to Wembley.

The date was 23 April 1995.

I know it's only the Auto Windscreens Shield but when you're Birmingham City it felt like the Champions League Final. Half of the Second City invaded the first, London. The long-suffering Blues fans turned out in their thousands. They would have happily taken any final of any sort as indeed would us commentators. Three trips in three seasons to the national stadium was fine by me. No Manchester United or Leeds United this time though, it was Carlisle United.

It was goalless after 90 minutes and was far from a classic, not that we were particularly expecting one. But a tension-filled extra half-hour was guaranteed because a sudden-death golden goal would decide a major final for the first time. Blues-mad Paul Tait scored it and it was one of those occasions when you could definitely say in commentary, 'There's no way back for Carlisle now.'

Tait tainted his triumph by revealing a t-shirt adorned with the words 'S**t on the Villa'. It caused uproar at the time in the Second City as you can imagine. That was Taity mind, I don't think he was ever planning to be a contestant on *Brain of Britain*.

Back in the league three days later Birmingham faced Brentford in what was effectively a title decider. Brentford were three points clear at the top. This game became another highlight of my commentating career as big Kevin Francis and trusty skipper Liam Daish scored in a 2-0 win amid an atmosphere that was absolutely ferocious.

St Andrew's was bursting with passion and plenty of it. A classic case of how fans can make a difference and the Blues fans did just that. The noise was incredible. When I think about that night now it still sends a shiver down my spine. It might even make it into my top five when it comes to awesome atmospheres at football grounds.

On the final day of that season Blues clinched promotion with a 2-1 win at Huddersfield in another extraordinary game. Weymouth old boy Steve Claridge scored his 25th goal of the season and Paul Tait struck, effectively, another golden goal to seal promotion. I think he kept his t-shirt under wraps that time.

That season with Birmingham City was a rollercoaster ride. I remember setting up all our technical equipment for commentary at York one day. Some local guy turned up and said we couldn't sit in our spot because, 'I've sat there for 43 years.' He could've easily helped by sitting in the row behind but he wasn't having it so we had to shift all our equipment. I suppose if you've sat watching York for 43 years you've earned the right.

It was like that at a few of the lower-division grounds. To amuse ourselves before kick-off we used to ask the locals which one Kevin Francis was as the team warmed up.

Kev was 6ft 7in and we knew who he was but it was surprising how many folk went to the lengths of pointing him out. It made us chuckle anyway. Little things, etc.

Barry Fry was a laugh a minute, maybe even less than a minute. He used to do a live radio interview with us just before kick-off at every game. The climb from pitch level to Middlesbrough's press box is a steep one. As presenter Tom Ross said 'We'll shortly be hearing from Barry Fry,' you could already hear Barry in the background shouting, 'You never f***ing told me it was this far up. I've had three bloody heart attacks, make that four any second now.'

Skipper Liam Daish wrote in his newspaper column that competition for places was important and nobody should feel secure of their place in the team. Daish was dropped for the next game with Fry exclaiming, 'I read his column and thought bloody right, what a f***ing good idea.'

Louie Donowa was a surprise sub one day having been on loan at Walsall. 'I didn't know he was coming back,' said Barry. 'I thought I'd bloody sold him permanently.' But then Barry did like a big squad. When I was doing my research in preparation for Blues games I'd have information on 30 or 40 players just in case one of them emerged from the wilderness.

I bumped into Barry a few years ago on holiday in Vilamoura on the Algarve. We were reminiscing about his time at Birmingham and he said, 'I was a lucky bugger to manage a club like that, I really was.' He may think so, but he was probably just what Birmingham City Football Club needed back then. He put them back on the map, one way or another!

There would be even better times ahead for the Blues. I so hoped club legend Trevor Francis would lead them into the promised land of the Premier

League but it didn't quite happen for Trev and that's such a shame because if you'd ever met him, you'd have wanted it to happen.

Steve Bruce eventually took them into the top flight and kept them there for a while, re-igniting the Second City derbies too in a favourable way for the Blues.

I was delighted when in 2011 Alex McLeish guided them to League Cup glory by beating Arsenal. I wasn't quite so happy that they beat West Ham in the semi-finals but if anyone knows how to lose a League Cup semi-final my team does. We were still at it, cocking up a semi-final!

A mix-up in the Arsenal defence allowed Obafemi Martins to score a last-minute winner at Wembley. Birmingham City lifted the League Cup and I suspect, for all the suffering the Blues fans had endured over the years, that one moment made supporting them worthwhile.

Until that is, to the end of the very same season when the Blues went and got themselves relegated from the Premier League. Almost as a punishment for actually winning a trophy. It could only happen to them. Well, actually, it could probably happen to West Ham too if we tried hard enough.

On the final day of the 2013/14 season Birming-ham were staring at relegation to the third tier again, as had happened in Barry Fry's first season. They trailed 2-0 at Bolton but remarkably recovered to snatch a draw and survive with an equaliser from Paul Caddis deep into stoppage time.

I was working on a later game at Everton that day and had parked up in Stanley Park ahead of my match. I couldn't get out of my car though. I had to stay and listen to the finale of Bolton v Birmingham on the radio. I cheered when the Blues pulled off the greatest of great escapes.

I have a soft spot for them and their supporters. I see a lot of West Ham United in Birmingham City, if you know what I mean. It must be something to do with the loyalty, the general despair and the suffering!

One thing's for sure, never has 'Keep Right On to the End of the Road' been a more fitting club anthem. A perfect match with Birmingham City Football Club. Bless them and KRO Blues fans.

7

Remember the Name

THE West Midlands was, and still is, a terrific football patch and it wasn't all about Aston Villa and Birmingham City.

We also covered West Bromwich Albion, Wolves and Walsall. West Brom weren't up to much at the time but as mentioned before they gave me the opportunity to work with not only the great Jeff Astle but also Tony 'Bomber' Brown, who still works on the same radio station in Birmingham. I have the highest regard going for Jeff and Bomber. True gents.

They could play a bit too. I've already spoken about Jeff but Bomber scored 279 goals for Albion. Say no more!

The Albion managers at the time I covered them were Keith Burkinshaw, Alan Buckley and Ray Harford and they were all no-nonsense but likeable men. That said, Buckley had a short fuse now and again and wins my personal award for the longest wait for a post-match interview.

After one Saturday afternoon game he kept us waiting until 6.10pm in the freezing cold tunnel at Huddersfield having lambasted his players in the dressing room for nearly as long as the match's duration! Even better, by that time he wasn't much in the mood to speak for long!

Ray Harford was Kenny Dalglish's assistant when Blackburn Rovers won the Premier League in 1995 and later went on to manage them himself. Ray had the kind of face that made him look like a miserable so-and-so but that was far from the case. He was one of the funniest men I've met in the game. Sadly Ray died of cancer at the age of just 58. A big loss to the game and a big loss to good old humour.

Walsall often loitered in the lower divisions. Yet they provided me with one of the games of my life, with more than a little help from Torquay United.

The date was 12 December 1995.

It was an FA Cup replay on a cold, cold night at the Bescot Stadium in the shadow of the mass concrete of the M6 motorway, which I'm sure added to the cold factor. I'm talking freezing, biting, bone-chilling. As presenter Tom Ross and I sat virtually encased in ice in a small and not very comfortable press box I'm pretty sure we could have listed a million places we'd rather be.

We weren't expecting much. Torquay were bottom of the entire Football League and Walsall were mid-table in the division above them. But it's often the games you least expect to be a classic that turn out to be a classic and this was certainly the case. Even to this day I can still barely believe what I witnessed that night.

It was all fairly innocuous for a while, and it was 1-1 at half-time. But things soon started to happen. Strange, weird, crazy things. Torquay went 2-1 up but Walsall equalised. Torquay went ahead 3-2 but Walsall equalised again.

In the last minute of normal time Torquay hit the post and the ball spun straight across the line, hit the other post, and somehow stayed out. Just as well it did, not for Torquay alas, but for us neutrals who were about to experience a continuing and amazing goal-fest.

To extra time and the second most astonishing 15 minutes of football I've ever seen (there's a bit of Celtic v Rangers to come later in the book).

By the end of the first period of extra time it was Walsall 7 Torquay 4. How did we go from 3-3 to 7-4 in a matter of minutes? It was breathtaking. There was just the one goal in the second period – we felt a bit cheated by that – as Walsall ran out 8-4 winners. It just goes to prove, never judge a game by its matchday programme cover. I never felt the cold by the way.

Anyway, enough of such career high points like that extraordinary night. One thing you're often asked as a commentator is whether you've ever made a huge cock-up. What's your worst mistake?

I never quite understand the public's fascination with that because the answer is an inevitable yes. Oh yes. You better believe it.

Graham Taylor was in charge of Wolves when I covered them. He's had to put up with a lot in his career after failing with England but that shouldn't mask the fact that he did have considerable success at club level.

I've always liked Graham because as a nervous young reporter at Capital I once went along to interview him when he was managing the country. I did a one-on-one interview lasting seven or eight minutes in which he was really open and forthright, having been under pressure at the time.

I was quite proud but as I went to turn off my tape recorder at the end of the interview I realised I hadn't actually turned it on in the first place. Oh no! I hadn't recorded it! What a twat! I'd ballsed up big-time and knew I couldn't go back to the office with nothing to show for my trip to an England press conference. There was only one thing I could do.

I explained to Graham that I'd made a complete arse of things and he was brilliant. He came back and did the whole interview again and yes I did check about 50 times that this time I was recording it.

Failing to record an interview with the England manager is pretty high up on my list of cock-ups but I've done worse in actual commentary, much worse.

I had an absolute nightmare during a game between Oldham Athletic and Aston Villa at Boundary Park. It just had to be there didn't it, scene of West Ham's St Valentine's Day Massacre. I could easily go off that place.

I had flu. Serious flu, not just mere man flu. It was a horrible, cold wintry day and believe me Boundary Park is unforgiving on a day like that. To be honest it's fairly unforgiving on a bright summer's day! Our commentary position was right at the back of the stand just behind the last row of Oldham fans. They could hear every word and they're not a shy bunch.

I kept having to reach down under the desk into my bag for medicine. So when Guy Whittingham scored to put Villa ahead I virtually lost my voice. After swigging some medicine I just about recovered to continue commentating.

A couple of minutes later I gave it 'so it's Oldham 0 Villa 1 here at blowy Boundary Park' at which point the Oldham fan directly in front of our commentary position beckoned for me to take my headphones off as he had something to say. Oh, he had something to say all right. 'The goal was disallowed mate. Offside. It's still 0-0 mate.' It sounded even worse coming in that blunt Oldham accent.

It's hard to dig yourself out of that mess on air. 'Er...actually it's still 0-0, sorry for misleading you for a couple of minutes there,' is never going to sound great is it? No way out. Sometimes you just have to hold your hands up. Shit happens in any job. It was only radio at the end of the day. Nobody got hurt, apart from me and my pride and a few thousand Villa fans who thought their team was ahead. Ooops.

On another occasion I was commentating on Birmingham City who had a player called Jonathan

Hunt. We used to update listeners with all the goal news from the other games so the producer's voice was constantly in my headphones, passing on those scores and scorers.

That was second nature for commentators, hearing someone talking to you as you were talking to listeners, but it required total concentration. The one point I lost concentration was when I was trying to remember a score the producer had passed on while at the same time trying to say 'Jonathan Hunt cuts inside'. You can probably guess the rest. It came out as 'Jonathan Hunt c*** er…cuts inside'. Once again, no way out. He wasn't that bad a lad to be honest. Ooops. Double Ooops. Triple Ooops.

I can't remember if I immediately apologised for using the C-word on air but I would hazard a guess not because I was too busy laughing, or positively corpsing in fact. I had to cross to our reporters around the grounds to regain my composure. Although every time I looked at presenter Tom Ross alongside me it just set me off giggling again. For most of that afternoon I was still chortling and tittering like a schoolboy who'd just sworn for the first time. What a pro eh!

Then there was the time when I fell ill during a play-off game between Bolton and Wolves at Bolton's old Burnden Park Stadium. I'd eaten a dodgy tuna sandwich from a garage and as the evening game wore on I felt more and more nauseous.

Tom had to do most of the talking that time (mind you he was a natural at that!) while I tried desperately to fend off that horrible feeling of imminent embarrassment. Typically of course there was a late goal which meant extra time. Extra worrying time about being sick. I so could've done without that.

Also, the press box at Burnden was tight and cosy and I had visions of chundering over many of my media colleagues. That seriously scared me but I somehow got through another 30 minutes without puking.

Bolton won in the end and were delighted when the full-time whistle was blown, but not as bloody delighted as I was. I had wanted Wolves to win as our local club but I'm not sure I'd have got through penalties without the re-appearance of that tuna sandwich in some format or other.

I never had a tuna sandwich for the next 18 years but have recently rediscovered them and quite like them. Well, you can't let these things get to you eh. Not for too long.

After those embarrassing moments on radio, I'm amazed I had managed to wangle some television work but I got lucky in that respect. In the early

1990s I was on the breakfast shift at Capital Radio and noticed in our office diary that there was a lunchtime function at Scribes, a club owned by Terry Venables in west London.

Having been up since 4am I didn't much fancy it but nobody else was around or available. Even so I tried to evade it but was told by the management that someone had to represent Capital there and that someone had to be me.

The function was the official launch of Sky Sports's Premier League coverage and I'm rather glad I went in the end. I ended up sitting next to Vic Wakeling, a no-nonsense but likeable Geordie who was in charge of Sky Sports. The big chief nonetheless. After a few glasses of wine, in me not him, I started pestering Vic for work!

My commentating experience was fairly limited by this point yet here I was giving it large, 'Remember the name Vic, I'll be commentating for you one day.' I blame it on the combination of wine and a 4am start. Okay, mostly the wine.

Vic must have wondered how he'd ended up sat next to a vaguely inebriated job-seeking pest whose commentating experience pretty much added up to half a Barnet v Carlisle match.

A few weeks later I either wrote to Vic or rang his office. Probably both. Amazingly he offered me some commentaries on the Bundesliga which I could fit in around my Capital work. I was still learning the commentating ropes (not that you ever stop learning). I was a rookie for sure. Vic and his number two Andy Melvin took a gamble and for that I owe them quite a lot.

It was a great experience on the Bundesliga working with presenter Peter Hutton and a top producer in Ian Condron, who now looks after Jeff Stelling and Co. on *Soccer Saturday*. My co-commentator was Alan McInally, who played for Bayern Munich (just in case he's never told you). Although I'm pretty sure he was injured during most of his time there. Sicknote!

There was never a dull moment when McInally was around and there never has been to this day. He would be on the telephone to the Bayern dressing room on matchdays to get the latest team news from his former team-mates. He was a big pal of Klaus Augenthaler in particular but could name-drop a good few others too! That was definitely the most impressive way I've ever got hold of a team's formation. Direct from the dressing-room.

I'm not sure we'd be able to get hold of Philipp Lahm, Thomas Muller or Robert Lewandowski just before kick-off these days, although I wouldn't actually put it past McInally!

Bearing in mind my radio cock-ups I thought I did well to successfully commentate on Uwe Fuchs and Stefan Kuntz in the Bundesliga around that time. Although I was probably smirking as I did so.

Not long after Sky Sports kicked off its Premier League coverage it threw me in on a couple of live games. Imagine the BBC doing that, taking such a big chance. Mind you, in this instance the BBC might have had a point.

I nervously mumbled my way through Crystal Palace v Chelsea and Wimbledon v Crystal Palace and I commentated like I was on radio rather than television. Mind you I still do that today sometimes!

Initially I thought I was ready for it. Well you do when you're young and full of it don't you? I've heard some of the lines I used during those two games since and it makes me cringe. I used the sort of corny stuff that worked well on radio at the time because that was our style, but they never seemed so suitable on TV. I don't know why, it was just a different world.

My humbling experience was a bit like Barnet v Carlisle revisited but you live and learn. If I had my way, I would banish the tapes of those two games and also ask the Premier League to remove all evidence of them from their results history!

Sky Sports also covered the Victory Shield, a schoolboy tournament involving the home nations, England, Scotland, Wales and Northern Ireland. I was asked to commentate on it one year and what a year to pick; 1995. The year one 15-year-old playing for England stood out more than any other, by a considerable distance. A boy by the name of Michael Owen.

In the England-Scotland decider played at St James' Park, Newcastle, the Scots had levelled at 1-1 when from the restart Owen took the ball, ran past any Scot in sight and scored the most unbelievable of individual strikes. Of course there would be a few more glorious goals for him to add to his collection in the years to come but that effort on Tyneside was truly remarkable.

I think I uttered the words 'Michael Owen – remember the name' over one of his other goals in that Victory Shield season. Although when I occasionally hear it back now it seems to have been merged over that wonder goal at St James' Park. By the magic of telly editing. Fine by me!

Another commentator used the 'remember the name' line when Wayne Rooney burst on to the scene with that cracking goal for Everton against Arsenal. I reckon I got in first though I might be kidding myself on that as I guess one of the older commentating guys had probably used it before. I won't be claiming the copyright but I'll keep pretending I did the original if you don't mind. As I've said before, little things please little minds.

Michael Owen scored a dozen goals during that schoolboy season. Wes Brown played in the same team. They beat a Brazil side at Wembley that included a lad called Ronaldinho.

Three years later Michael scored another great goal. This time it was in the World Cup against Argentina. I followed his career closely and he's now a co-commentator for BT Sport. Strangely he appears to get a fair bit of stick which seems to go with the territory these days but I think he sounds good. Mind you I may be biased. I still see a vision of the extremely polite 15-year-old I interviewed and commentated on. The boy done well.

8

Merry Christmas Fergie

THE date was 28 December 1997.

I commentated on a remarkable game at Highfield Road, Coventry City's old stadium. The Sky Blues were trailing 2-1 against Manchester United with a few minutes remaining but then gave away a penalty. Dion Dublin equalised. 'Dublin is bubbling' I uttered. Another line that would have sounded better on radio that I quickly regretted using on television. In fact, come to think of it, it may have sounded rubbish on radio too. It was good to know I was learning so slowly!

Suddenly Darren Huckerby scored a wonderful winner, a stunning solo strike. I do love a bit of alliteration. The sort of goal that is so easy to commentate on. He did the tricky bit, darting round a few defenders en route to goal but not just any defenders, Manchester United defenders.

I screamed 'sensational' – a word that has served me rather well over the commentating years. I consider it simple but effective which is often the best way. Anyway by United's supreme standards, it was an unthinkable late collapse.

After the match I had to interview Alex Ferguson. I usually enjoyed that particular challenge but can't say I was overly looking forward to it this time after they'd tossed the game away in ridiculous fashion. From 2-1 up to 3-2 down in a matter of minutes, late minutes. Although strangely Fergie generally had more to say after a defeat than a victory. Maybe because he didn't suffer many. It was something different to talk about.

The BBC reporter went first but at the end of his interview murmured, 'I've been asked by the office to ask you a question we're asking all managers today and that is, what did you get for Christmas Alex?' I'm guessing they were planning a funny montage at the end of the show relating to managerial gifts. It must have seemed like a good idea at the time when floated around the *Match of the Day* office. But time had moved on.

United had just let a 2-1 lead slip in the dying minutes. They'd been handing out presents themselves and as far as Fergie was concerned Santa was out, Scrooge was in. It was more no, no,no than ho, ho, ho.

The interview room at Highfield Road was tiny and I'd squeezed in at the back while Fergie was standing by the opposite wall near the door. I was close enough to see he was hardly full of festive cheer. I sensed he might do a runner in response to that question and he sure did.

Off he went down the corridor and by the time I'd wriggled clear of cameramen, sound men, lighting lamps and wires he'd disappeared back inside the United dressing room. Amid his rage he'd obviously forgotten he'd agreed to do an interview with me. Oh great. Bloody great.

I tentatively knocked on the dressing room door hoping nobody would actually hear it. It must have been the softest knock ever in the history of knocks on doors but one of the United backroom boys actually opened it to a trembling commentator giving it 'er…um…er…Alex said he'd do an interview for Sky'.

Fergie soon appeared with a face like thunder, and possibly lightning, but he seemed to take pity on the nervous wreck at the door. As we walked back to the interview room he muttered, 'Was it me or was that a bloody stupid question?' to which I said, 'It was stupid but it was just someone's idea in the office who maybe hadn't thought it through under the circumstances.'

As he seemed vaguely genial by now I tried to inject some humour into the proceedings. 'Mind you, that's buggered up my first question,' I said. He looked at me as deadpan as deadpan can be and snarled, 'Just get on with it boy.' I did and he gave an excellent interview in defeat again. And probably to annoy the BBC a bit.

I covered another Coventry v Manchester United match at Highfield Road just after Ferguson's first autobiography had been published, in which he was less than complimentary about Gordon Strachan, who was Coventry's manager at the time. Prior to the post-match interview Fergie made it as clear as clear can be that, 'If you ask any questions about the book I'll f*** off out of here.' I think he made his point rather well. Clear and lucid.

Strachan arrived separately in the interview room a few minutes later with, 'You look like a nice young man, you're not going to ask anything about the book are you?' In this instance, Gordon was ahead on charm, I'll give him that. I was itching to start both interviews with, 'So, about this book then...' but I resisted. I kind of suspected I'd be the only one who thought that would be remotely funny.

I never received the full blown hairdryer treatment from Fergie. Obviously my questions weren't anywhere near challenging enough! I've seen others on the receiving end and it was a sight to behold. I feel I missed out on something there, although I'm not complaining too much. I came quite close though.

The date was 29 January 2000.

Referee Andy D'Urso awarded Middlesbrough a controversial penalty at Old Trafford. The United players, led by a snarling Roy Keane, surrounded D'Urso and it all looked extremely unsavoury. Half a dozen United players circled the official. It became one of the stand-out images of the season.

In the immediate aftermath I had to interview Fergie post-match. I seem to recall it went something like this:

ME: What did you make of the penalty incident?

HIM: It wasn't a penalty.

ME: What about the reaction from your players?

HIM: Well they reacted because it wasn't a penalty.

ME: Might their reaction be considered over the top?

HIM: It's not a penalty. Not. A. Penalty.

At that point he gave me The Stare. The famous Fergie Stare. I didn't see it many times myself and I'm quite glad about that because it was piercing. A stare to make your bones shudder. If looks could kill. And there's a good chance death might be instant. I reluctantly moved on to another line of questioning. Someone said to me after, 'I thought you might have pushed Fergie a bit more.' As they say in Scotland, aye right.

It was always a challenge interviewing Fergie and if you put your foot in it you knew he'd take advantage. I didn't mind that, I quite liked being kept on my toes. There was a lighter moment when Teddy Sheringham joined, at the time, an elite band of players to score 100 Premier League goals. He did so with a hat-trick against Southampton. Fergie interview time again.

ME: Alex, what can you say about Teddy Sheringham, who's become one of an elite band to score 100 Premier League goals?

HIM: Has he? Is that right?

Now at this point he's naturally got me wondering if I'm right. Fergie knows every statistic going about everyone and everything in football. Absolutely nothing passes him by. His knowledge was on a par with Big Ron's all those years ago in La

Coruna. No danger. Surely he must've known about Sheringham's imminent century? I decided to stay confident about it even though my insides were churning at the thought I'd cocked up.

ME: Yes, his second goal was his 100th.

HIM: Really? You sure about that?

At this point, no not at all actually Alex but I've come so far I can't turn back.

ME: Yes definitely.

HIM: Well if that's the case it's a remarkable achievement.

I suspect he was having me on, winding me up. If so, it was a roaring success for him. I was on the phone to the office straight after the interview to make sure I'd got it right. I had. Phew!

After another game at Old Trafford I saw Roy Keane giving an interview to the Irish station RTE. I'd never interviewed him before so thought I'd try and claim an interview too. As he finished with RTE I quickly cut across him with, 'Roy, any chance of an interview with Sky?' It was a bit like that in the interview area. You had to be quick to get your man.

Keane stood still but ignored my request so I tried again. He stood still but ignored me again even though I was stood right next to him. Surely he must have heard me. Oh he had all right. After one further attempt he stepped towards me, came very close to my face and growled, 'PLEEEAAAASSSSSE. How about a please?' He then uttered, 'Manners…honestly…shocking manners.'

I thought it was ironic because I hadn't seen much in the way of decent manners from him when out on that pitch but this was off the pitch where players are different. I found myself asking him again, 'Any chance of an interview? Please!'

Maybe he actually had a point. In the adrenaline rush to nobble him for an interview I never did say please but I was fairly delighted anyway to be told off for bad manners by Roy Keane. What a player, what a leader of men, what a leader of teams. If anyone is going to tick me off then let it be one of the best players I've ever seen.

United's next game was against Real Madrid in the Champions League and at the end of the interview I sarcastically said, 'Thanks very much for the interview Roy and good luck against Real.' He smiled and went, 'Oh, thank you very much,' not realising that I was trying to take the piss. I thought at the time if I ever write a book that story is going to feature. There it was.

On yet another visit to the Theatre of Dreams I had a nightmare trying to interview David Beckham. He'd signed a new deal with United that very day. ITV's veteran reporter Gary Newbon was loitering with intent in the tunnel and would stay there all game whereas I had to head up to the television gantry to commentate.

Beckham was injured for the actual game so Gary was able to secure an exclusive interview during the match while I was busy commentating. Gary wasn't shy about letting me know about it either as I arrived for the post-match interviews. The challenge had been set!

I accosted Beckham three times with a rather pathetic, 'If you've done an interview with them you've got to do one with us as well.' A weak argument on reflection but I was desperate!

I failed miserably with Gary chortling in the background but I didn't mind that too much. I liked Gary, one of TV's great characters. He often talked about himself but then he had sure had some stories to tell. He made me laugh.

As I was picking my bag up to leave Old Trafford that day there was a tap on my shoulder. I turned round to see Beckham standing there sporting a big smile. 'I just wanted to say I'm really sorry again.' Typical of the man, he even let me down in a nice way. What a gent.

I was fortunate enough to commentate on quite a few of United's 3pm Saturday kick-offs in the year they won the treble and there were more of those back then than there are now. I can think of worse places to be on a Saturday afternoon.

I loved going to Old Trafford and that team of 1998/99 were an absolute joy to watch. They may have left it late in the Champions League Final against Bayern Munich but I'm glad they turned it around to claim that amazing treble. I remember a vintage United display from the following season too.

The date was 1 April 2000.

Guess who were going to be the April Fools, not for the first time. Yes, my team, West Ham United. Why was I not surprised?

The Hammers took an early lead through Paolo Wanchope. The Costa Rican had scored a dazzling goal at the same venue on his debut for Derby a few years earlier. He obviously liked the place and should have actually made it 2-0 a few minutes later although frankly a 3-0 or 4-0 lead might not have been enough on that day and even 5-0 is questionable.

United turned on the style. Paul Scholes helped himself to a hat-trick, including a cheeky yet supremely skilful back-heel. David Beckham floated a fabulous free kick in off the underside of the bar, which always makes it look better.

'That was brilliant, that was breathtaking, that was Beckham,' I screamed. I was happy with that line. It was the moment I forgave him for blanking me on that interview! It was hard for a commentator to go wrong in that game as United ran out 7-1 winners, playing some spectacular football. There was just so much to eulogise about.

I actually forgot my team were on the receiving end, as I often did when commentating on them. I just admired such a complete performance from United and it was one of those very rare days as a commentator when there wasn't much I could've called better.

I think I pretty much nailed everything. Even if I say so myself. So there.

There's usually something you think you could have said or should have said in a commentary. You are always striving for perfection, even though you are ad-libbing for 90 minutes. It's not like there's a script. Not like you can go back and do it again. Not like you can give it, 'Excuse me Becks, could you take that free kick again fella, I didn't quite call it right the first time.'

On that particular day though I was at commentating peace with myself. Sorry West Ham that it had to be you. But thank you Beckham and Scholes. Thank you Fergie. I couldn't have done it without you. Oh and I'd better say thank you to Roy Keane too.

My favourite Fergie story takes me back to West Ham many years ago. There was a great guy called Jim who used to stand on reception at Upton Park greeting visiting teams and anyone else who came his way. He was a typically straightforward East End guy who worked there for years. His wife also worked at the club on matchdays and was a smashing lady too. She used to make me cups of tea galore when I worked there as the stadium announcer.

When Jim died, Fergie sent a letter of condolence to his widow's home. It meant the world to her. That was the unseen side of the man. He did a lot of similar things over the years but never felt the need to particularly publicise it. He was undoubtedly Mister Angry many times during his management years but that was part of his make-up. He really could be a very decent man. He was certainly a very decent manager. Thanks for the memories Sir Alex and Merry Christmas to you.

9

That Is Sensational

O LD Firm. Two words that will always send a shiver down my spine, back up it and back down again. And that process may be repeated several times. There is nothing quite like the big Glasgow derby in my book, and this is my book.

I've commentated on over 40 frenetic encounters between Celtic and Rangers. Or should I say Rangers and Celtic? That's how it gets to you, try not to upset anyone. Although that is easier said than done.

The best Old Firm game for me was always the next one. Bring it on. They met at least four times in a season, possibly more if they collided in the cup competitions which they often did. The more the merrier as far as I was concerned. One season they met seven times and many reckoned that was too much to take. Not me, I'd have happily taken more.

Sure it was a fixture that came with too much baggage, far too much, but as a sporting occasion it is something else, a unique experience. For me there is nothing, anywhere, to match the awesome atmosphere and sheer intensity of an Old Firm game.

I was fascinated by the Glasgow derbies in my younger years living in Dorset. It all seemed a long way away from me. Both teams had exceptional players back in the day and even their kits looked great, side by side in the tunnel and when going hammer and tongs out on the pitch. Blue and white. Green and white. There's just something about it.

Funnily enough I noticed that Celtic didn't have any numbers on the back of their shirts in those days, just on their shorts. I thought that must be rather tricky for commentators. Don't get me wrong, commentators would know the players inside out but sometimes if you can't quite see something or if you are making a difficult call you want the reassurance of seeing that number.

I'd often wondered what it would be like to go and watch an Old Firm game but never did. So my first experience of this feisty encounter would be while commentating on it.

The date was 20 September 1998.

It finished Rangers 0 Celtic 0 at Ibrox but it wasn't an ordinary goalless draw. The Old Firm don't do ordinary.

There were a fair few chances and the noise was deafening. I remember the Rangers goalkeeper Lionel Charbonnier made a terrific save from Henrik Larsson. The game flashed by. It really did seem to be over in an instant. I may not have had any goals to call but I wasn't too bothered. I was hooked on the Glasgow derby. And the goals would come. We may as well cut to the chase eh?

The date was 2 May 1999.

Celtic 0 Rangers 3. The day Rangers clinched the title at Celtic Park. The far extremes of agony and ecstasy. The unthinkable as far as Celtic were concerned but Rangers had been thinking about it a lot. Neil McCann, later to become a Sky Sports colleague, scored twice but that wasn't even half the story. Or possibly even a quarter of it.

Celtic's French defender Stephane Mahe was sent off after half an hour. You wouldn't have got great odds on Mahe seeing red, he always looked a bit crazy in those fixtures, and in most other games in fairness!

In the aftermath referee Hugh Dallas was struck on the head by a coin and pictures of blood dripping from the cut flashed around the world. A couple of fans invaded the pitch trying to get near the ref. Another fan fell from the top tier to the bottom and was giving it large on the signal front as he was carried away on a stretcher. It was complete and utter mayhem. Pure pandemonium.

Just when you thought the atmosphere couldn't possibly become any more poisonous, Dallas gave Rangers a controversial penalty immediately after his gashed head had been treated on the pitch. Jorg Albertz scored from the spot to add to the carnage.

There was so much inexcusable disorder that day it was frightening. The mark had not so much been overstepped it had been stamped on several times and smashed to pieces. Although, as bad as it was, I couldn't help thinking the worldwide audience of millions watching the game probably bloody loved it.

The Old Firm met again later that month in the 1999 Scottish Cup Final at Hampden Park. Everybody was on their best behaviour. It was as tame a Glasgow derby as I've seen. Rangers won again just to rub their rivals' noses well and truly in it. Spectacular revenge would be coming for Celtic but they'd have to wait until the summer of 2000 when Martin O'Neill strode into Glasgow.

Martin was a fascinating character, and still is. I had covered many of his games at Leicester and can't remember a game, or indeed a post-match interview with him, that I didn't enjoy. He had a terrific team at Leicester's old Filbert Street stadium. A team that included Neil Lennon, who would follow O'Neill to Glasgow's East End and eventually into the hottest of managerial hotseats.

I knew we would be in for some interesting times under O'Neill. I certainly expected sparks to fly in his first Old Firm match. The sparks flew all right. Here there and everywhere on one of the most extraordinary days in the history of this unrivalled rivalry.

The date was 27 August 2000.

A date etched on the minds of Celtic fans everywhere. It was quickly tagged the Demolition Derby. Celtic were 3-0 up after just 11 minutes. I'd never known anything like it. Well, Walsall 8 Torquay 4 had a bizarre quarter of an hour but this was at a rather different level.

It was 100 miles an hour, and some. Trying to keep up with the frantic pace and blistering tempo of that devastating spell of football was hard work for me on the TV gantry but possibly even harder for Rangers on the pitch. And there was more to come. So much more.

It's one of the few matches I've commentated on that I've watched back in its entirety. I don't much like the sound of my own voice but it had been such a helter-skelter ride of a game I had no idea if I'd actually done it justice. I couldn't actually remember much of what I said. This is pretty much what I did say.

As the teams entered the field I said, 'Old Firm games...sometimes unbelievable...often uncompromising...always unmissable.' I knew it was a game that didn't really need to be given the big licks. I was often accused of over-egging a game that spoke for itself but, what the heck, I quite enjoyed stoking the fire. Little did we realise what astonishing drama lay ahead, from the very first minute.

1-0: 'And it's turned in by Chris Sutton. Unbelievable. Chris Sutton makes an immediate impact on his Old Firm debut and Celtic are in front.'

2-0: 'Celtic are seeking a second. And they have a second! It's Petrov and it gets better and better for Martin O'Neill and Celtic. A quite incredible start.'

3-0: 'And they're queuing up here. It's another one...for Paul Lambert...and in paradise this is the stuff that Celtic dreams are made of.'

Celtic Park is known as Paradise as all their fans will tell you. But I actually meant to say 'in the place they call Paradise' to explain it to those who might not know. Celtic fans still kindly quote that line to me to this day which is very humbling but I still wish I'd said, 'In the place they call Paradise.' I know, I should have got over it by now. Anyway, there was quite a lot going on, that's my excuse.

Rangers got a goal back through Claudio Reyna and then had a Rod Wallace strike wrongly disallowed so it could have been 3-2 by half-time and had it been who knows what might have happened next. You couldn't have ruled out anything on a day like that. As it turned out what happened next was one of the best goals I've ever seen.

4-1: 'Larsson…oh he's in…Larssonnnnnnnn… that is sensational…he missed all four Old Firm games last season but he just loves making up for lost time. World class.'

Co-commentator Davie Provan summed up Larsson's breathtaking chip perfectly, 'A very special goal from a very special player.' Rangers responded again to make it 4-2 but Larsson hadn't finished with them yet.

5-2: 'Petta delivers…Larsson's header…he's done it again…it's a double for Henrik Larsson… it's number five for Celtic.'

Barry Ferguson was then sent off for Rangers. It wouldn't be an Old Firm game without a red card. I remember Neil McCann getting booked for nearly slicing Jackie McNamara in half. They're now the best of mates ironically!

6-2: 'Have Celtic got another one left in them? Yes, they have. Sutton scores. Six of the best for the very best today…Celtic. Chris Sutton, who started it all, finishes it all.'

So, not bad for starters for Martin O'Neill. 'We could play for another 100 years and not get a start like that ever again,' said the Celtic manager. Rangers boss Dick Advocaat held his hands up, 'Quite simply we have to give all the credit to Celtic. The scoreline doesn't lie.'

Dutchman Bobby Petta was flying on the flanks for Celtic and tortured his fellow countryman Fernando Ricksen, who was making his Old Firm debut. Fernando had stayed in the same hotel as me when he first signed for Rangers and we ended up having a beer in the bar. I took an instant liking to him and not just because he bought me a beer.

I was telling him about the Old Firm games but he responded in a very Dutch way by saying, 'I've played derbies in Holland too. Not a problem.' I told him this would be like nothing he had ever experienced but he seemed sceptical.

Fernando was subbed early in his first Old Firm game after Petta had turned him inside out and was sent off in his second Old Firm game. He soon got the hang of them after that though. It seems he lived quite a life off the field, and sometimes on it, but Fernando always took time out to say hello and have a chat after that initial beer. He came across as a decent man.

It was heart-wrenching to see Fernando suffering from Motor Neurone Disease although typically he decided to do battle with that too.

There was no argument over the goal of 'The 6-2 Game'. Henrik Larsson's chip summed him up perfectly, a phenomenal player. I'm amazed he stayed in Scotland as long as seven years but Celtic can have that sort of pulling power and I'm rather glad he stuck around. And no that doesn't make me a Celtic fan, steady on. It's just that he was pure gold to commentate on. He made my job easy.

Larsson cost Celtic a bargain £650,000 from Feyenoord in 1997. On his debut he gave the ball away at Hibs and it led to the winning goal. He scored an own goal on his European debut for the club. It wasn't a sign of things to come. Larsson scored 242 goals in 314 games for Celtic with 53 of them coming in one mind-blowing season. He even propelled Celtic to the UEFA Cup Final in 2003 which they came so close to winning. It was a privilege to see him on the Scottish stage for so long.

Larsson could've played in one of the big leagues long before he did but typically and fittingly he later went and helped Barcelona win the Champions League in 2006. They were 1-0 down to Arsenal but he came on as a substitute to set up two goals. How very Henrik. He'd earned the right to that kind of glory. He even fitted in a brief spell with Manchester United too and naturally made an impact there as well.

I'm often asked who's the best player I've ever commentated on in Scotland. I don't know why people bother to ask. I can't imagine many Rangers fans would argue with me over Larsson. Okay, maybe one or two would!

Lubomir Moravcik was a pretty good watch too. He was 33 when he arrived at Celtic which begged the question: what the heck had he been doing with his career?

The skilful Slovakian had spent eight years in France with St Etienne and Bastia. Either he was a very late developer or someone missed a trick there. Lubo rarely missed one himself.

Three months after 'The 6-2 Game' the Old Firm conflict continued when they met at Ibrox.

The date was 26 November 2000.

Rangers had been toiling after that early-season hammering at Celtic Park and were a massive 15 points behind their rivals. So of course it only went and finished Rangers 5 Celtic 1.

Barry Ferguson started the scoring but after a Henrik Larsson equaliser £12m man Tore Andre Flo scored the most crucial of the goals to put Rangers 2-1 up. Flo was never worth £12m in 12 million years but at that moment everyone of a blue persuasion probably thought he was.

Ronald de Boer, Michael Mols and Lorenzo Amoruso completed the rout. A 5-1 win after a 6-2 defeat. You couldn't make it up. Only in Glasgow.

Two of the most intense derbies I commentated on were played in the same month in 2008.

The scheduled New Year Old Firm clash had been postponed following the shocking and tragic death of Phil O'Donnell, who collapsed on the pitch playing for Motherwell. An absolute gentleman, an awful loss.

It transpired that Celtic would host Rangers twice in the space of 11 days. They were behind Rangers in an absorbing race for the title but not for long.

The date was 16 April 2008.

In the first encounter, the man from Japan, Shunsuke Nakamura, scored a long-range stunner which nearly caught me out on the gantry. I was waffling about something else right up to the moment he decided to smack it goalwards. It was a proper screamer. Nakamura was always a good watch. I loved commentating on him and not just because I could easily extend his name in commentary. The same goes with Nacho Novo.

1-0: 'Nakamuraaaaaaaaaaa! His first Old Firm goal and typically it's a beauty.'

1-1: 'Isn't that just typical too from Nacho Novoooooooo.'

Rangers then had defender Carlos Cuellar sent off for handling on the line. Allan McGregor saved the resulting penalty despite hobbling with an injury. He'd been subbed by the time Celtic scored an amazing 93rd-minute winner.

2-1: 'They've done it! Jan Vennegoor of Hesselink answers a Celtic SOS – Save our Season – they are still in the title race and yet again it's a case of better late than never under Gordon Strachan.'

Big names in big games and Jan certainly had the biggest name of the lot. I did a Hearts v Celtic game once that I should never have done because I had a serious throat infection and I sounded terrible. Some would say no change there. Commentators never say no because we don't want to let anyone else do the game but I was seriously struggling to speak. So I also knew that Big Jan would score the first goal. He did. I couldn't really call him Big Jan so I went for the full version. It nearly finished me off.

The date was 27 April 2008.

Could the Old Firm repeat such drama 11 days on? Of course they could. It was my birthday and the game was a gift to commentate on, the best present ever.

1-0: 'A startling start to this final Old Firm game as Scott McDonald puts Celtic in front after just over three minutes.'

McDonald was actually offside so the assistant referee would've been rather pleased when Rangers soon changed the terms of engagement.

1-1: 'David Weir was in the thick of it and he's claiming it and Rangers respond quickly.'

1-2: 'And it's in from Daniel Cousin and Rangers have turned this game on its head.'

Of course there was far more drama to come, as always in an Old Firm showdown. It was Celtic's turn to show their powers of recovery.

2-2: 'McDonald….it's in …and McDonald claims another goal. It's 2-2 just before half-time. This is incredible.'

3-2: 'One big kick…Barry Robson…he makes his mark at Celtic Park…and this topsy turvy tussle takes another twist. Celtic are in front again in a must-win match for them.'

Celtic had thrust themselves back in the title race and with Rangers juggling a remarkable run to the UEFA Cup Final that year, Gordon Strachan's side secured the title on the final day with a win at Dundee United.

You can't beat a good title-clinching game. I remember in 2007 Celtic had been taking their time in securing the title but a win at Kilmarnock would do the trick. It was 1-1 when Celtic were given a last-minute free kick and Shunsuke Nakamura was stood over it. I knew he was going to score. I'm no prophet, I think everyone in the ground just had the feeling of inevitability. I promptly milked the moment, just a bit.

'Everyone inside Rugby Park, everyone watching at home, in pubs and clubs, around the world is holding their breath. If anyone can do it, he can. Nakamuraaaaaaaa…he has done it! Isn't that just typical. What a way to win the title and how fitting that the goal should be scored so late and should be scored by Shunsuke Nakamura. They've had to wait for their title but good things come to those who wait. Celtic. Champions.'

Quite often when commentating on football I try to brace myself to be ready for anything by expecting the unexpected. You don't want to be caught out or taken by surprise. But not in that one moment in time. I totally expected it and if you can't think of a half-decent line when you know what's coming you shouldn't be commentating. Cheers Naka.

10

A Twist in the Tale

MANY assume that Celtic 6 Rangers 2 is the best Old Firm game I've ever commentated on. I always name it as my joint-favourite and not just because I'm about to level it up with a Rangers triumph! Okay, maybe that does have something to do with it actually. It's safer that way!

The date was 4 May 2002.

I think it was BBC commentating legend Barry Davies who once said that there's no such thing as a perfect commentary. I know where he's coming from but as mentioned earlier I was pretty happy with myself after Manchester United 7 West Ham United 1, if not with my team.

I was about to experience my Scottish version of as close as you can get to commentating contentment. It was the Scottish Cup Final but no ordinary final because it was an Old Firm final. Yes, them two again.

Rangers beat Celtic 3-2. Sorry Celtic that you had to be on the receiving end but I wouldn't take it too personally. I wasn't overly bothered when my own team had been pumped 7-1 at Old Trafford as I wallowed in the personal glory of a commentary where all my lines seemed to fall into place.

Commentators can be a selfish bunch, especially in the quest for perfection, especially when perfection usually comes along as often as a West Ham trophy lift.

As the action commenced at Hampden Park I gave it large:

'Anything can happen and it probably will. You can't predict the unpredictable but you can expect the unexpected.' Not unless Nakamura had been playing back then and sizing up a free kick anyway.

The beauty of giving it the big build-up like that was that you absolutely knew this was a fixture that would definitely live up to the billing. That was never in doubt.

Big John Hartson gave Celtic an early lead but Danish striker Peter Lovenkrands usually saved his best for derby day in Glasgow.

1-1: 'Mjallby's header might give Lovenkrands a chance...and he has taken it. What a response from Rangers. Peter Lovenkrands...he always scores against Celtic.'

He hadn't finished yet but giant defender Bobo Balde restored Celtic's lead before Rangers bounced back again.

2-2: 'It's Barry Ferguson...oh yes...the captain shows the way with a fabulous free kick. Rangers were never going to give up easily. You never can do when the Old Firm meet.'

Extra time was beckoning but Rangers weren't planning to go the difference as Lovenkrands popped up in injury time. If you're going to take the lead for the first time in a cup final, do it in injury time.

3-2: 'Amoruso...here now is Neil McCann...is there going to be a twist in the tale? Lovenkrandssssss! Yes there is! Peter Lovenkrands...it had to be him... he has surely won the Scottish Cup for Rangers. Lovenkrands...a man on a mission...a mission to win that cup...an extraordinary end to a captivating cup final.'

Barry Ferguson lifted the world's oldest national trophy as I uttered, 'Ready is the word on the Rangers club crest and they were ready today. Ready willing and able.'

It had been a spectacular encounter. I think my contentment centred on the winning goal. I'm told that some Rangers fans later produced a t-shirt with 'Is there going to be a twist in the tale' printed on the front and 'Yes there is' on the back. Although I never saw one, probably just as well they didn't send me one to wear.

I got lucky. I had probably asked the question 'is there going to be a twist in the tale' many a time over my commentating career and usually there wasn't. Nothing actually happened. I was due a twist and what a twist it was.

The date was 31 August 2008.

Another standout Rangers success on derby day came on this day with a 4-2 win at Celtic Park. Kenny Miller had tasted both sides of the divide and always seemed distinctly unfazed by that. He obviously didn't go out in Glasgow much!

Kenny scored twice on his return to familiar territory but the goal of the game came from Pedro Mendes. Steven Davis took a corner and zipped it back to Mendes some 35 yards out. He couldn't could he? He could.

'That. Is. Just. Brilliant.' I screamed. I went into a full stop frenzy, making every word sound like a sentence. I've no idea why, maybe it was to buy me some time to think of something to say about such a stupendous strike. I've. Done. Quite. A. Lot. Of. That. Since. Too.

I remember another 4-2 victory for Rangers at Ibrox in 1999 when Argentine striker Gabriel Amato scored. I used to love it when he did because he's got one of those names that you can drag out forever as a commentator. Amatoooooooooo!

There have been quite a few names like that over the years in Scotland. I've been spoilt for choice. I've already mentioned Nakamuraaaaaaa and Novoooooo. Then there was Amoruso, Reyna, Flo, Porrini, Prso and Sebo. Although I never had to shout the latter's name out too often!

I quite like rolling the name Claudio Caniggiaaaaaaaaa too and what a guy he was. He didn't come to Scotland for a holiday that's for sure. He gave it his all. When he first came over and played for Dundee I remember standing in the derelict Dens car park eating a rhubarb crumble from the Sky food wagon with director Davie Carton.

It was pissing down and all of a sudden Caniggia parked up, got out his car, walked over the rough ground and skipped past us giving it a 'hi guys'. What a way to interrupt a rhubarb crumble. Claudio Caniggia at Dens. Things you never thought you'd see in your life. Surreal.

Celtic had a good few names you could extend to. Bellamy, Viduka and my personal favourite Hooperrrrrrrr. You could add a bit on to Suttonnnnnn, Hartsonnnnnnn and Larssonnnnnn too. It's a commentator thing.

I mentioned Celtic clinching a title at Kilmarnock in the last chapter. So it's only fair to mention Rangers clinching a title in this chapter. I know, the balance is beautiful.

The date was 15 May 2011.

Kyle Lafferty scored after 46 seconds at Rugby Park and that certainly set the tone. Steven Naismith added a quick second and then Lafferty struck again in a devastating early blitz on the Killie goal.

0-3: 'Rangers setting their stall out with a serious statement of intent here…oh they're in again…Jelavic…to Laffertyyyyyyyyy (oh good another name to drag out)…he's scored again… this is incredible…this is remarkable…this is extraordinary. Wrapping up the title in no time.'

Rangers won 5-1 in Walter Smith's final game in charge. It was his 21st trophy with them. What a way to go for one of my favourite guys in the game. I miss him!

Handily my two favourite Old Firm matches featured a win each for Celtic and Rangers. Phew. I know it looks like I'm sitting on the fence but it would have been hard to separate 'The 6-2 Game' and 'The 3-2 Game'. Okay, I am sitting on the fence really and you know what? I would happily stay perched there.

I used to love the accusations of bias levelled at me before but mostly during and after Old Firm duels. It went with the territory and most of the time I took it as good banter. Although a death threat once upon a time possibly overstepped that old mark again.

Fans in Glasgow, and indeed across all of Scotland, are never shy of telling you what they think. Why should they be? I don't mind that. I love the passion of it all. It does amuse me that some of the most fiercely biased fans in the world often accuse me of the one thing they are. Biased!

A popular complaint is that I sound more excited commentating on *Celtic goals compared to Rangers goals/Rangers goals compared to Celtic goals (*delete as applicable depending on who you support).

I challenge anyone to find any concrete evidence of that. I think you'll find I was as excited about Henrik Larsson's wonderful chip as I was about Peter Lovenkrands's dramatic winner.

I still get grief from some guy on Twitter now over my commentary of Ugo Ehiogu's winner for

Rangers at Celtic Park in 2007. Ugo scored with an overhead kick and this guy reckons I didn't do it justice. He actually has a point.

I was a bit low-key on it but having seen Ugo play for many years at Aston Villa I never knew he had an overhead kick in him so maybe I was just shocked! Or maybe I was just having a crap commentary day. It can happen. Either way a memo to guy who keeps tweeting me about it. It was over eight years ago. Get over it! Move on!

Mind you I'm a fine one to talk. I'm not really over that FA Cup Final foul on Paul Allen, or Tony Gale's red card, or George Reilly's winner for Cambridge bloody United.

If I had a pound for every Glasgow cabbie who's asked me whether I'm a Rangers man or a Celtic man I reckon I'd currently be sunning myself on a big yacht in the Bahamas. I answer West Ham and nobody believes me. I try Weymouth but that doesn't quite work either.

The fact is I am a complete neutral when it comes to the Old Firm. I just know some people will still be shaking their heads now. I genuinely love them both. Why wouldn't I? A country bumpkin from Dorset who moved to London and then to the Midlands. I never had a connection with Glasgow's Big Two and I'm quite glad about that now.

I can appreciate them both. Two huge clubs. Two great stadiums. Two great words. Old Firm. My spine is tingling again. I want them back together again.

Sadly one of the greatest rivalries in world football was put on hold for nearly three years when Rangers went bust in 2012 and were demoted to the bottom division. They didn't meet again until 1 February 2015 in a League Cup semi-final that was predictably one-sided and almost surreal because Celtic were so far ahead of Rangers as was to be expected.

I wasn't commentating on the game but was planning to go along to Hampden Park to watch. I changed my mind. It didn't feel like a proper Old Firm game after such a long wait and with the two clubs in such contrasting positions in their history. It will take a while for Rangers to get back on a level footing with their old rivals. They've been through so much, too much in my personal opinion.

At the very most Rangers might have shunted down to the second tier for a season, assuming they bounced back up immediately. The shocking decision to send them down to the bottom division and start all over again is something I still can't get my head around. Talk about shooting ourselves in the foot in Scottish football.

I found it rather unsavoury that the smaller clubs in Scotland ended up deciding the destiny of a great institution like Rangers Football Club. Especially as those clubs knew they'd be getting a piece of Rangers on their way back because they were guaranteed big crowds at home and a couple of trips to Ibrox.

I would actually have kept Rangers in the top flight at all costs and found other ways to punish them because quite simply the Old Firm match should have been kept alive. It's the one Scottish game everyone around the world wants to watch. Sometimes we have to look at the bigger picture. Yet we somehow managed to get rid of the Glasgow derby for a few years. The watching world remains baffled by that.

Rangers could have been given a huge points deduction and maybe financial penalties that would've benefitted the other top flight clubs. From where I was looking too many revelled in their bitterness towards Rangers. They saw it as a chance to get one over the big boys who'd been misbehaving. If it had been Celtic in such trouble I'm guessing the reaction would have been similar. It even came down to a question of morals. I'm not sure football has ever been wholly into morals in a big way.

A few Celtic players have spoken out about missing Rangers and the Old Firm games. Good on them. They usually get a bit of stick for doing so but they're only telling the truth. Celtic have strolled to titles in the absence of their biggest rivals. You can only beat what's in front of you and Celtic have done that.

Take a look at those men in Hoops though, captain Scott Brown in particular but others too like Kris Commons, Craig Gordon and Leigh Griffiths. Winners one and all. They want to be doing battle with Rangers. They want to be tested to the full and pushed to the limit.

Those are the sort of games that would be the highlights of their domestic careers. No wonder they miss them.

It must be hard to get yourself up for run-of-the-mill league matches that you know you are going to win before a ball is kicked. Even if you don't there's plenty of margin for error anyway. It's not like anyone is seriously breathing down their necks like Rangers invariably were.

When even the Scotland manager Gordon Strachan is saying the leagues should be revamped to ensure we get Rangers, Hibs and Hearts back in the top flight you know how serious it is. Good on Gordon for speaking out.

I've certainly missed commentating on a huge club like Rangers. I did a few of their games in the bottom two divisions and had to pinch myself. Was I really watching Rangers having to play at some of these places? I can only imagine what the players and fans were thinking.

We did their first league match outside the top flight, at Peterhead, who nearly beat them. It was all so very strange. It wasn't pretty but it was effective as Rangers coasted to back-to-back titles but escaping the Championship proved harder work as Hearts rebuilt and regrouped to greater effect.

It's sad that so many people seemed to take such great pleasure at the demise of Rangers. I still receive tweets saying I shouldn't call them Rangers or refer to their history because they're not called Rangers and they haven't got a history. Spare me.

It was all such a sorry state of affairs that did nothing for the perceived image of Scottish football outside of its own boundaries. Wherever I go, whether elsewhere in the UK or abroad, there is total disbelief that we've suspended the Old Firm rivalry.

Sure, Rangers should've been punished, but did we really need to go that far? To such ridiculous lengths? I know many will not share my views on that but hey, it's a game of opinions. It would be boring if we all had the same ones. Rather like it would be boring if all commentators sounded the same.

All I can say is I can't wait for the day Rangers return to the top flight and I know I'm not alone. I can't wait for the day they become a major force again either. That may take some doing but in the meantime, just get them back for goodness sake.

11

Wow! Wow! Wow!

I LOVE the word 'wow'. It's small but perfectly formed and effective in a wonderfully simple kind of way. I've screamed it across a few matches over the years, firstly I think when Gary McAllister fired in a stunning 35-yard strike while playing for Coventry City. That may have even become a 'wowwee'!

However, only once have I ever screamed it three times at the end of a game, bang on the full-time whistle. I felt this particular match was worthy of the accolade.

The date was 7 November 2012.

Celtic were hosting FC Barcelona in the UEFA Champions League. You might remember it.

A fortnight earlier Neil Lennon's Hoops had nearly nicked a point at the Camp Nou or Nou

Camp if you prefer. Whichever way round it sounds like a right good place. Although the television gantry there is actually so high up the players look like dots on the pitch. The ball usually joins up those Barca dots mind!

Normally I would moan about the view from afar but when you're in the Nou Camp there is nothing to moan about is there? Get on with it and enjoy the experience. They could put us even further away and I wouldn't mind. It's the Nou Camp. It'll do for me.

Giorgios Samaras was a handful on European nights that season and he gave Celtic an early lead. Andres Iniesta equalised on the stroke of half-time with a wonderful team goal. What else would you expect? I exclaimed, 'It's fantasy football for real.'

After levelling at such a crucial time Barcelona looked nailed on to ultimately see off Celtic in the second half but a colossal and outstanding defensive performance kept them at bay until injury time when Jordi Alba snatched a winner. You couldn't argue that Barca deserved it for their dominance but Celtic had put so much into the game.

So to the return fixture in the east end of Glasgow. There is nothing quite like Celtic Park on a Champions League night and their faithful followers really cranked it up a notch or two, or three or four that night, just when you thought they couldn't possibly get any louder.

As the two teams walked out of the tunnel I could sense we were in for a night to remember. I never talk when the teams emerge from the tunnel on a night like that. There is no need. The noise from the crowd carries the moment. There is nothing I could add to the thunder of Celtic Park.

I also always make a point of not talking over the Champions League anthem as the teams line up before kick-off. That's the time to let the music roll and to let the fans do their bit again. That piece of music never fails to send a shiver down my spine.

I wasn't expecting Celtic to win but I did expect them to have a right good go and give Barca something to think about at least. They always raised their game on a Champions League night and by a considerable level. Anyway, whatever happened we all had the chance to watch Lionel Messi and Barcelona play again, never a bad thing. Oh, and Iniesta and Xavi. And a few more besides!

Victor Wanyama headed Celtic in front and although I screamed his name I think I got drowned out by 60,000 fans going absolutely potty.

'That moment when a dream becomes reality. Celtic have only gone and taken the lead against Barcelona…again!'

I was quite happy with that line, if you don't mind me saying. There's nothing worse than not being happy with your first goal call in a game. You want a decent line to set the tone for the commentary.

If you make a mess of your first goal call, if you're just not happy with it, it preys on your mind for the rest of the game. It's a bit like if you fluff your team news at the top. It could be a sign of fluffs to come. I'm not as insecure as I've just made myself sound, honest.

Celtic were far from insecure themselves in the company of Barcelona greatness. They only went and doubled their lead as young Tony Watt broke away towards goal, striding along as if he didn't have a care in the world.

'This is Tony Watt. He's done it. This is the stuff of legends. At the age of just 18 Tony Watt takes his place in Celtic folklore. This is mind-blowing. This is Celtic 2 Barcelona 0.'

Barca got a goal back through Messi at the end but Celtic held on for one of the most famous victories in their history. It was an unforgettable night that made headlines around the world.

Celtic fans have again been very kind about my commentary that night which is humbling but those are the easy games. There was just so much to say and I always thank the players because when they perform like that it's hard for a commentator to go wrong.

Although actually, I did go wrong. I didn't mean to put an 's' on the end of 'legends' because I think technically I should have said 'the stuff of legend'. I know you might think I'm being harsh on myself but that's life for a commentator. It bugged for me for a while but I'm over it now. Maybe.

The trouble for Tony Watt was that the best moment of his career had come at the age of 18. He's never going to be able to top that.

Sadly Tony was later sent out on loan to Belgium and is now at Charlton. There's a player in there and I hope he has a decent career. His name will forever be remembered by everyone connected with Celtic and by everyone fortunate enough to be present on that extraordinary November night. Matches like that do not come along very often. Those really are the games of our lives.

There were a few other matches in Scotland that were probably worthy of the 'wow' factor and you'll probably be amazed that none of them involved the Old Firm. I'm guessing fans of clubs outside the Glasgow giants are probably thinking I've carped on enough about Celtic and Rangers. They might have a point.

The date was 22 October 2000.

A couple of months earlier Celtic had walloped Rangers 6-2 in the Glasgow derby. Ooops. I've just gone and mentioned them again. Sorry. Now it was time for the Edinburgh derby and incredibly that finished 6-2 as well. What were the odds on that I wonder? Not that I imagine anyone had placed such a bet.

Mixu Paatelainen scored a hat-trick for Hibs who were managed by Alex McLeish and they were a good watch at the time. They certainly were on that day. I feel a bit for Mixu because even though he scored three goals it's the sixth goal that is remembered the most, scored superbly by Russell Latapy.

6-1: 'Latapy…twisting…turning…scoring…a lovely one-two…that is absolutely wonderful from Russell Latapy.'

I always like to balance things up in Scotland, whether it's in Edinburgh or Glasgow or anywhere else come to that. So now for a Hearts triumph!

The date was 19 May 2012.

For the first time in its long and illustrious history the Scottish Cup Final was an Edinburgh derby. Hibs hadn't won the cup since 1902 and were fed up hearing about it. Was it their destiny to finally triumph against their city rivals? They soon got the answer. No. A big fat NO.

First and foremost as a commentator you want a close competitive contest to talk about. If that's not going to happen then you want an absolute pumping and thumping because that then becomes a story.

A 2-0 scoreline is rather dull after all but 5-1 gives you more to play with on the television gantry. I've already told you us commentators are selfish creatures that way.

'Darren Barr seizes the moment, seizes the cup final. It's Hearts who strike first on Edinburgh's day of destiny.'

That was a sign of things to come as Hearts got the steamroller out and, inspired by the talented and so very watchable Rudi Skacel, absolutely flattened their old rivals. Hibs were utterly humiliated and I suspect they will be taunted about it for many a year. I tell you what though. I so hope Hibs win that bloody cup one year soon because I want to be there to call it!

I've commentated on 15 Scottish Cup finals but Old Firm and all-Edinburgh finals apart most of them seem to have been pretty routine results. I did miss the 2008 final when Rangers beat Queen of the South 3-2 mind so no surprise it was half-decent. I was in New York getting engaged so I'll blame the wife for that one.

I've seen some storming semi-finals over the years though. I remember in 2003 when Rangers beat Motherwell 4-3 in an enthralling tie at Hampden Park. I'd been doing a game at Ipswich the day before and was booked on a flight from Stansted to Glasgow that evening.

Alas this was a time when the need for photographic evidence when you checked in was being introduced by some airlines but not others at that time. I'd normally used an airline that didn't insist on such evidence until later but this was a different airline and they did insist on it. I did have some photo id but not the photo id they wanted to see and the jobsworth check-in girl steadfastly refused to let me on the plane despite my pleas. I was virtually on my knees but she was merely enjoying my agony I think.

Oh shit! I was stuck in Stansted at 9pm on a Friday and needed to be at Hampden around 12 hours later.

I decided I would hire a car and drive up but it was Easter weekend and the only hire car left at Stansted Airport was a bloody huge Mercedes. I couldn't even work out how to get the thing started but once I did I was on my way up the M1 and M6 arriving in Glasgow in the ridiculously early hours. I must have had about two hours' kip so I'm glad

Rangers and Motherwell served up some goals or I might have fallen asleep.

I've had so many travel issues over the years I swear I could do a pretty good remake of the classic movie *Planes Trains and Automobiles*. I would also revel as *The Hotel Inspector* on TV although Alex Polizzi is rather good at it too and looks a whole lot better than me, by a distance.

I was bang on time for an eye-catching semi-final weekend in 2013 when Falkirk roared into a 3-0 lead against Hibs and should've made it 4-0 only for Hibs to launch an astonishing second-half comeback to triumph 4-3. Did that mean Hibs' name was finally on the Scottish Cup? Nope. Don't be silly, of course not. The very next day Celtic also won their semi-final 4-3 against Dundee United and promptly trounced Hibs in the final. 'The 4-3 Weekend' was rather fun.

Two years later Falkirk and Hibs met again at the semi-final stage. Hibs dominated and Falkirk won 1-0. That's why football can drive you mad. Inverness Caledonian Thistle beat Celtic 3-2 in the other semi-final which was an epic encounter overshadowed by The Hand of Josh. Caley Thistle defender Josh Meekings clearly handled a goalbound effort on the stroke of half-time but the officials failed to spot it.

Celtic were rightly raging as they could've been 2-0 up against ten men before half-time, assuming they scored the penalty. Meekings was later retrospectively banned for the handball but won his appeal in a rare victory for common sense. It was quite sad that an honest mistake by officials led to such a furore and Caley Thistle had a decent shout for a penalty later too. Maybe these things do even themselves out.

Amid the considerable controversy Inverness were probably the better team over the piece but Celtic had been denied a treble, no wonder they were incensed.

That made it a hat-trick of Scottish Cup wins for Inverness over Celtic. In 2000 they famously won at Celtic Park. In 2003 they beat them 1-0 in the Highlands. Now they had done it again. It wasn't the story Celtic wanted to hear but it was a story and a half.

It would take a very special game in Scotland to top an Old Firm match. So Motherwell and Hibs, take a bow.

The date was 5 May 2010.

Hibs had lost their last six matches prior to this one. Motherwell had lost five of their last six. So, although both teams were still chasing a European place, I can't remember being particularly enthused

170

about this match when I arrived at Fir Park a few hours before kick-off.

But then all those years ago I'd felt exactly the same about Walsall v Torquay and that finished 8-4. I never ever thought I would see 12 goals in a game again. I was wrong.

Hibs raced into a 4-1 lead in the first half with Colin Nish helping himself to a hat-trick. John Sutton pulled one back for Motherwell but Anthony Stokes struck two quick goals to extend Hibs' lead to 6-2 with less than half an hour remaining. What we then witnessed was nothing short of phenomenal. We may never see the like again.

Giles Coke and Tom Hateley soon made it 6-4 and then John Sutton headed home for 6-5. It was pure crazy and was about to go off the scale. Hibs goalkeeper Graeme Smith clattered into Lukas Jutkiewicz. Penalty to Motherwell. Smith went and saved Ross Forbes's spot-kick. You couldn't make it up. It looked like that was that. It looked like Motherwell had blown their big chance for an astounding comeback. Oh no they hadn't.

6-6: 'Jutkiewicz on the chase…and he might get there…Hanlon is with him…Oh wow! Ohhhhhh wowwwww! It's the comeback of comebacks. It's Motherwell 6 Hibs 6 in the game of the season, the game of a few seasons.'

Jutkiewicz's spectacular strike was compared to Marco Van Basten's famous goal in the European Championship Final of 1988. I'm not sure it's quite up there but it certainly isn't far off.

On the full-time whistle I said, 'Unreal. Unbelievable. Amazing. Incredible. Astonishing.' At which point I think I ran out of words to describe what we had just seen. Although I don't much like the sound of my own voice you might not believe me because of what I'm about to say. I still frequently watch that game back on YouTube, more than any other game. I think I just want to be sure I got the score right.

Motherwell had slashed ticket prices to try and entice more fans to come along. A tenner for adults and kids for a quid. I think they got their money's worth. They should have told the new fans they'd attracted that it was like that every week. If only it was. It finished 6-6. Six bloody six. Wow! Wow! Wow!

12

It's Not the Taking Part That Counts

I T'S not the taking part that counts, it's the winning. I used that line a few times ahead of Old Firm games and also before Football League play-off finals. Partly because, as you may have gathered, I quite like the line but also because it's so very true. Especially where the Championship play-off final is concerned. It is a match worth millions. A coveted place in the Premier League is at stake. The result is everything. Absolutely everything.

In the 2013/14 season Derby County should have triumphed in the final at Wembley yet Queens Park Rangers snatched an undeserved late winner and ended up in the Premier League. Just like that.

There's the proof. Just win it, any which way you can.

That was so cruel on Derby, who are one of my favourite clubs. I love Pride Park and I know it's not called that anymore but it is for me. I love the fact that they sell out week in week out regardless of what division they're in or who they're playing and their fans make some right good noise. The Premier League needs them back as soon as possible.

I was the main commentator on the Football League from 2002 to 2006 and the end-of-season play-offs were clearly the highlight and always eagerly awaited. The play-offs have been magnificent for football. In my first season I was fortunate enough to do a game that will linger long in the memory of everyone present. It still lingers in mine.

The date was 15 May 2003.

The place was Bramall Lane. Sheffield United and Nottingham Forest were level at 1-1 going into the second leg of their semi-final. Forest strolled into a 2-0 lead and looked on course for the final but the Blades had a terrific spirit about them and, with manager Neil Warnock barking on the touchline, they weren't about to lie down.

They recovered to 2-2 and forced extra time. With eight minutes left in the additional half-hour

Paul Peschisolido scored a terrific goal to complete an astounding comeback.

3-2: 'Peschisolido…he's finding a way…doing what he does best….Paul Peschisolidoooooooo (yet another name to drag out!)…Sheffield United's extraordinary season takes an extraordinary twist. They were 2-0 down now they're 3-2 up…Forest thought they were going to Cardiff…now Sheffield United think they are.'

I'd known Pesch since he first arrived in England as a young lad at Birmingham City, long before he became Mr Karren Brady! He ripped his shirt off to celebrate. I could've done without seeing his bare chest right enough but it was a big part of the moment as Bramall Lane went wild. Another of my favourite stadiums. You can so feel the passion. Another club we need back in the big time.

We hadn't finished yet though. Forest legend Des Walker put through his own net, but then so did Rob Page at the other end. It finished 4-3 to Sheffield United although it had been such a crazy night I had to double check it before saying the scoreline on the full-time whistle.

I loved seeing my co-commentator Chris Kamara jumping up and down with excitement, living and loving every goal, every kick, every moment of drama. I know Kammy is enthusiastic about most things in life but I'm sure he took it to a new level that night and no wonder, what a fantastic football match it was.

With Wembley out of action the play-off finals at that time were played at the magnificent Millennium Stadium in Cardiff, which by the way is also high on my list of favourite stadia. Whoever designed that wonderful arena should take a bow. It puts so many other venues to shame. The fans were right on top of the action, creating an atmosphere that is among the best I've witnessed in football. It was certainly a perfect place for those kind of high stakes matches.

The date was 26 May 2003.

I quite fancied Sheffield United to pip Wolves to a place in the Premier League. My prediction was way off course, no change there. Mark Kennedy, Nathan Blake and Kenny Miller put Wolves 3-0 up before half-time. Kenny Miller – now there's a man I've seen a lot of in my commentating career. He was always good for a 'Millerrrrrrrr' shout too!

Early in the second half Wolves goalkeeper Matt Murray saved a Michael Brown penalty. Had he not done so I might have fancied Warnock's Blades for another epic comeback but Wolves' time had come.

Full-time: 'Wolves are in the Premiership. Dave Jones is the man who has taken them into the big time. I'm sure their fans will want to hear those words again, Wolves are in the Premiership. After 19 years away after 19 years of hurt the Wolves are back. And about time too.'

The date was 25 May 2003.

Cardiff City and Queens Park Rangers met the same weekend for the right to return to what was then the First Division, now the Championship. Cardiff won 1-0 in their own city. Andy Campbell scored a dramatic winner in extra time.

Full-time: 'After 18 years in the bottom two divisions they've finally made it out. A sleeping giant no more. The Millennium Stadium in Cardiff belongs to Cardiff and this could be the start of something special. For years they were going nowhere. Now they're going somewhere.'

This might be a strange choice as one of my favourite games but the tension that day was unbearable as both sides slogged it out for the big prize. I was completely wrapped up in that occasion from start to finish. It wasn't a classic football match yet it gripped me from the off and never let go.

Lennie Lawrence was in charge of Cardiff and I discovered that his partner actually worked at QPR. A good line. I double-checked that with Lennie and it was true but he said he'd prefer I didn't use the line. So I didn't. What a spoilsport!

Cardiff went on to even better things further down the line, probably because they didn't have to face the Super Terras of Weymouth again to knock them out of their stride!

The date was 30 May 2004.

It was a similar story to Cardiff v QPR the following season when Brighton beat Bristol City 1-0 to win promotion to the second tier. The immense turnout for that final showed the enormous potential of both clubs. Brighton had been playing at the Withdean Stadium, a crumbling athletics venue which I absolutely despised, although not as much as the Brighton fans did.

I was standing in manager Mark McGhee's ramshackle office there one stormy night when lightning struck the roof. It was quite scary but McGhee noted that it could only have caused thousands of pounds' worth of improvements.

I've since seen Brighton play at their sparkling Amex Stadium. It's a bit different. Good on them. I will always have a soft spot for them because of those tough times between leaving the Goldstone Ground and moving in at the Amex. The fans who stayed all the way through deserve a medal.

I quite like Bristol City too and whoever gets things right there will hit the jackpot. Steve

Cotterill looks like he could be the man and I hope so because he's a manager I've worked closely with over the years. It's good to see them back in the Championship but Bristol City are big enough for the Premier League. No pressure on you there Steve.

The date was 29 May 2004.

I've known Iain Dowie for a long time and he's a bubbly, infectious character. In December 2003 he took over a Crystal Palace side languishing at the bottom of the table. Five months later they beat West Ham 1-0 in the play-off final to book a place in the Premier League. Football eh…bloody hell (copyright Sir Alex).

Neil Shipperley scored the winner. He'd been on the same tube train as me when he made his Chelsea debut many years earlier. He was wearing his Chelsea tracksuit and I wondered who the heck he was as we made our way to Stamford Bridge. I soon found out when a couple of hours later he started the game. Good on him for taking the tube even if he was a bit of an unknown then. Maybe a few players should try public transport!

Full-time: 'Crystal Palace are in the Premiership. It's no longer a dream, it's reality. In the space of five months Iain Dowie has taken them from relegation possibles to promotion certs.'

After the game the match director said, 'Sorry it was your team that lost.' I can honestly say I hadn't thought about that. I was too busy focusing on the job in hand. It honestly didn't sink in till afterwards that my team had lost. I surprised myself there. I know, what a pro! However I was thinking about it a bit more a year later.

The date was 30 May 2005.

West Ham returned to the Millennium Stadium and 12 months on were triumphant this time, edging out Preston North End.

1-0: 'Etherington...Zamoraaaaaaaa (more name-dragging bliss)...he's done it this time... Bobby Zamora is the man of the moment...the man of the Millennium Stadium.'

I felt for Preston boss Billy Davies, who I'd known since he was in charge of Motherwell years previously. I know Billy annoyed a few folk at Nottingham Forest but he was always different class with me. Those wee Scottish guys love an argument now and again mind!

I was particularly delighted for West Ham boss Alan Pardew because I'd got on quite well with him from the very first time I met him while watching his Reading players train ahead of a game to get some inside information. At the end of training he said, 'Would you like some lunch, your belly looks like it might.' I quite liked his humour and it hasn't changed over the years. Nor has my belly come to think of it.

Pards invited me into the Hammers' dressing room after that win at Cardiff. Not quite so professional perhaps but I still went in and milked the moment like a schoolboy. Most of the players had left the dressing room by then but they'd left behind the sweet smell of success! Apologies for sneaking in there. I know it's not really the done thing.

Watford were under new management in 2005 and I covered them in the first week of the season in a Friday night match at Cardiff. I'm not sure I've spent enough time in Cardiff in my life! Adie Boothroyd had been given the Watford job and I didn't know him so thought I ought to make the effort. I arranged to meet him on the morning of the game at the hotel Watford were staying in just off the motorway at Newport.

Adie spoke impressively over a coffee and then came up with one of the best predictions ever, possibly THE best. Watford had struggled the season before and were expected to do so again. As I got up to leave Adie said, 'It's ironic our first away game is in Cardiff isn't it,' which I queried. 'Because that's where our last game will be in May. We'll be back here for the play-off final.'

I admired his brashness but didn't believe him for one minute. You guessed it. Nine months later Watford were indeed back in Cardiff, thrashing Leeds United 3-0 at the Millennium Stadium to win promotion to the Premier League. Never doubted you Adie.

Also during my stint on the Football League I was lucky enough to deal with some really good guys who won automatic promotion to the Premier League. As fun as the play-offs are, going up automatically, is better just in case you lose in the play-offs. If you could guarantee a play-off win you'd take that drama for sure but I know that's a daft way of looking at it!

Nigel Worthington took Norwich up as champions in 2004 and it really couldn't have happened to a nicer man, or a nicer club. We sometimes went into his office or the boardroom for some after match nibbles and a glass of wine. The food was fabulous but then with the lovely Delia Smith about so it should be!

I used to ring Paul Jewell for his Wigan team while he was travelling to the ground from his home on the high up Moors. A combination of a rubbish mobile signal on the Moors and Jewell's Liverpool accent ensured I never really caught his team but he was such a laugh to speak to I kept him talking anyway.

I spoke to Mick McCarthy frequently when he was taking Sunderland into the Premier League in 2005. I love Mick because what you see is what you get. I remember doing a lot of Sunderland games during their promotion run-in although every time I rang him on the morning of the game he seemed to be in the bathroom.

He genuinely was, it wasn't an excuse because he always rang back. I ended up speaking to his wife more than him. To be fair he does always look pristine. No wonder!

Gary Megson took West Brom up twice, in 2002 and 2004, but I'll always remember a conversation with him not long after when he said, 'I'm bored. I've been here for four years and the players are fed up of hearing from me.' He reckoned four years was about the best most managers could hope for at one club, with some notable exceptions. And some would just love to get anywhere near four years. I think Megson was pretty much correct.

Portsmouth were a terrific watch under Harry Redknapp with Jim Smith assisting. We were often invited in to their office and it was proper old school with Jim usually putting a bet on the horses before the game and sipping red wine after. The phrase 'one of the game's great characters' might have been invented for Jim.

I became quite close to Colin Lee when he was in charge of Wolves and Walsall, and he came up with one of the best lines ever. Away from football Colin was into property and was living in a stately home which he was renovating to sell on. I rang him one evening and the signal was iffy. He said, 'Try me at home. I'm just turning into my drive. I'll be at the house in 15 minutes.' I still laugh at that to this day.

I had first worked with Colin on a pre-season tournament staged at the City Ground in Nottingham. There were four teams involved with two games on the Saturday and two on the Sunday. I was covering the event for Capital Radio so it was very early in my career.

Alas on the Saturday night fellow commentator Dominic Johnson and I were rather bored. We were going to go out as we'd heard that Nottingham had a ratio of three girls to one man so we thought we might be in with a chance. I think they knew we were coming because the ratio didn't look that high as we hit a couple of bars. We returned to our hotel and rather overdid the wine before moving on to the Baileys. I know, it's not big and it's not clever.

I woke up with a hangover from a place below hell, a rug for a tongue and the feeling that I could vomit at any time and at some distance. I learnt a valuable lesson there and then. Never overdo it like that the night before a game. Sure, I like the odd glass of wine but I know when to stop. I know there's a job to be done. I know I shouldn't have needed to learn that lesson but I was a rookie learning the ropes and in any case it was obviously all Dom's fault!

Colin Lee was co-commentator on the Sunday and I let him do most of the talking as I munched on Nurofen. Never again! These days I can barely stay up past 11pm so there's not much chance of anything similar occurring.

The play-off finals are among the highlights of my commentating career but it wasn't all high drama in the Football League. The number of matches during the regular season made it a right old slog at times, for players and commentators. There's a surprising game that is high on my list of unforgettable matches, although not necessarily for the right reason.

The date was 15 February 2003.

It was almost certainly the coldest day in the history of Bootham Crescent. I seriously shivered through York City 0 Hartlepool 0 and the game didn't help. Normally you don't notice the cold when you're commentating. It hits you at the end of the game but this was such an awful drab affair that not only was I losing all feeling in my body, I was also losing my mind, thoroughly bored at the appalling lack of quality on show.

I focused on York right-back Simon Marples and decided that every time he touched the ball I was going to shout his name out as if he was about to score. I did it a few times until our producer Dave Wade told me to stop being silly. He had a point. I had even screamed 'Marplessssss' as he took a throw-in on the halfway line. I remember some of the fans below the gantry looking up wondering why the hell I was shouting.

So much for the professionalism of that day when Crystal Palace beat my team eh. This was more like the big kid that snuck in the West Ham dressing room at the Millennium. Cameraman Ian Tushingham was next to me on the gantry at York that day. Whenever I see him these days he still screams 'Marplesssss' at me. That's cameramen for you. Keeping a gag going forever.

I did a similar thing with John Nutter at Gillingham until another telling-off. Nutterrrrr! Little things please little minds for sure and very occasionally mine is minute. It's not all glitz and glamour and when it isn't you've got to have a laugh along the way, while still getting the job done. I had my professional hat on most of the time, honest!

13

Good Morning Walter

AS you may have gathered from the last chapter I have dealt with many a football manager over the years, and mostly the opportunity to speak to them and become close to some of them is one of the many perks of the job.

All commentators like to have an early shout on teams ahead of the game you are covering. That's just the way it's always been, anything to have a head start and to give those slow TV graphics folk more time to type the names in!

Some managers simply won't play ball on that front because they just don't want to tell you their team but a surprising number are quite helpful, as long as you keep it highly confidential.

This involves earning the trust of managers and ringing them early on the day of a game, or even the night before. Although I always leave it until the day of the game because managers are a strange breed (no wonder in that job) and there's every chance of a change of mind once they've slept on it.

So many managers have been hugely helpful to me since I started commentating. When Walter Smith was in charge of Rangers for the second time I used to ring him around 8.30am on a matchday. We'd have a little chat, put the world to rights in fact, he'd give me his team and that would be that. Some of our conversations were priceless but what happens in an early Sunday morning telephone call stays in an early Sunday morning telephone call. Shame really, because it could make up another entire book!

I've got a lot of time for Walter, a true gentleman, but like most managers I wouldn't have wanted to cross him. Let's be honest, they all need a bit of bastard in them to do what they do.

The backroom team at Rangers were top guys too; Kenny McDowell, Iain Durrant and goalkeeping coach Jim Stewart. No wonder Jim was a goalkeeper, he has the biggest hands of anyone I've ever met. I used to actually fear shaking his hand because I knew my hand was in for a serious crushing.

The one and only Ally McCoist was assistant to Walter and later succeeded him in the Rangers hotseat (and boy was it hot!). Coisty was similarly classy. He managed Rangers during the most difficult time in their history and it's hard to comprehend what he had to put up with off the pitch. If he ever gets to write a book about all the goings-on it would be quite a read. A lot better than this book for sure but then that wouldn't be hard.

Some will say he wasn't a great manager but under the circumstances it would be hard to fully judge him in my opinion. It may not have been pretty at times, but he mostly got the job done.

I remember meeting Coisty at the 2010 World Cup in South Africa when he was so excited about succeeding Walter. Little did he realise what lay ahead. He would have to manage Rangers through the most challenging of times where the football was often secondary to the financial turmoil. I bet he learnt a lot about things he never really wanted to learn about!

I did my first Scottish league commentary with Coisty back in 1998 so I will always have a soft spot for him. He's always been good to me but what I like most about him is that he's the same with everyone. He never changes, he probably never will. He's earned the right to a wee break after Rangers.

Martin O'Neill was harder to get to know, mainly because he was so intense on the day of the game. 'Martin's Matchday Mode' as I used to call it (MMM). He was completely and utterly wrapped up in what lay ahead.

The only time I never saw him out of 'MMM' was when he came up behind me in the tunnel, did that old kick in the back of my knee trick, and as I predictably collapsed he grabbed me round the waist and called me a fat bastard. He'd already secured a title to be that laid-back on the day of a game!

I was in the same hotel as Celtic one night before a game at Hearts and ended up having a couple of glasses of wine with Martin, possibly even more. I'd put that night down as one of the best I've experienced in my career because he was open, honest and an utterly fascinating character. Rather like with Walter, we put the world to rights. If there was someone to praise, we'd do it but if there was someone to slaughter, even better. Much more fun eh!

Alas, rather like with Walter's Sunday morning telephone calls, what's said in the Edinburgh Marriott stays in the Edinburgh Marriott. Although that would've been worthy of a few chapters too!

Martin appeared to pick his team rather late and even then changed his mind on occasions but once he got to the ground, once he'd been inside the dressing room to tell his players, he'd come back out to hand me a scrunched-up piece of paper on which he'd scrawled the Celtic formation for me. Thanks very much, that'll do nicely.

I love watching Martin in his role as a TV pundit because not only is he rather incisive, he's quite prepared to take on other pundits if he's not happy. He can be a very funny guy too. I wish him well with the Republic of Ireland although not at Scotland's expense, sorry Martin!

Martin had taken over at Celtic after a bizarre spell at the club which saw John Barnes managing the team with Kenny Dalglish returning as director of football. Neither were particularly forthcoming in giving us an early shout on the team whenever we did Celtic live.

However, we had a few player contacts in the dressing room and usually found out anyway. We would always endeavour to keep such information confidential but on one occasion someone from Celtic saw the formation written out on someone's notepad in the tunnel. We'd have got away with it but Paul Lambert had been ill overnight and had been replaced by Colin Healy. There's no way we would've known if someone hadn't told us. Ooops!

Celtic lost the match and apparently Barnes and Dalglish kept the players in the dressing room for ages afterwards trying to find the naughty mole. Nobody owned up and Dalglish later rang Davie Provan to request the name of the villain. It all seemed a remarkable overreaction.

We had hardly cost Celtic the game by knowing the team in advance. As far as I know the name of that mole didn't ever come out and it's not going to come out here either. I'm not telling you much in this chapter am I?! I never reveal my sources, though it was a really good source!

I know managers can be paranoid when it comes to opponents discovering their team in advance but we would never dream of passing on such information. It's not like we would go charging into the opponents' dressing room and post the team up.

In any case the players themselves are more likely to let things slip. Players talk to each other. They might be former team-mates now on opposing sides and they would be bound to gossip as to who's in the side. I'm quite sure a lot of the time players and managers would be pretty good at guessing the other team's line-up before they see the official teamsheet.

I remember frequently ringing Craig Brown for team news when he was in charge of Preston North End. He used to say, 'Which team would you like first – ours or theirs?' It doesn't really affect the outcome of the game at the end of the day. If only we had such powers! I'd have made sure West Ham won a few more games.

Martin O'Neill's initial rival at Rangers was Dick Advocaat, who came across a fairly brusque Dutchman, but I quite liked him for his no-nonsense approach. At one game Jorg Albertz was only on the bench which was surprising as he was in the form of his life. I asked Dick why and he said Albertz felt a minor hamstring twinge in training, but said, 'But for you Ian I will bring him on after 60 minutes. Sixty minutes exactly. Make sure you say it will happen.'

Well, there was an offer I couldn't refuse. I milked it in my pre-match team news smugly, saying, 'We expect Albertz to come on for the last half-hour.' Sure enough, bang on the hour, Advocaat made that very substitution as promised. Cheers Dick!

At one game I couldn't find Dick but his assistant Bert van Lingen was standing in the tunnel so I accosted him.

Me: Is that going to be a 4-4-2 formation Bert?

Bert: I can't say.

Me: Is Amato injured? I see he's not on the bench?

Bert: I can't say.

Me: Can I just confirm who your subs are?

Bert: I don't want to give you that information.

Me: Who's on penalties?

Bert: I don't know.

Me: Thanks a lot for your help Bert.

Bert: What? But I didn't help at all.

Indeed. I don't think Bert did irony.

When Craig Brown was in charge of Scotland he used to give me all the scouting reports and DVDs of the opposition and that was particularly invaluable if you were doing the Faroes or San Marino when perhaps your knowledge of players might have been a little sketchy. Craig would give me all the information he would later relay to his players. You can't ask for more than that!

Alas Berti Vogts wasn't quite so forthcoming during his disastrous reign as Scotland manager. After one game he refused to speak with a couple of our reporters who had previously upset him by asking a fairly standard question. So I had to hot-foot it from the gantry to the interview room after the match to be the latest to have a try.

It was a year to the day since Berti had been appointed so I asked, 'How far do you think you've come in the year you've been in charge?' Berti took exception to that too, quizzing me with, 'Why are you always looking in the past?' Maybe it was better than saying, 'Not very far at all.'

It's a shame the Scotland job didn't work out for George Burley because I'd become quite close to him during his time at Ipswich, Southampton and Derby. Terry Butcher worked with George and he was another I had and would spend a lot of time with. Terry must be due honorary Scottish citizenship having spent so much time up north, although that famous blood-spattered picture of him in an England jersey might still cost him such an accolade.

I've only fallen out with one manager over the years although I think we're both over it now and just as well because he's the current Scotland boss! Gordon Strachan's Celtic were losing 2-0 at Hibs who played some fantastic football under Tony Mowbray. I said Celtic were 'well and truly put in their place' on the second goal. Celtic actually recovered for a 2-2 draw.

The morning after the game I picked up a message on my mobile. 'It's Gordon Strachan, ring me.' I didn't think he was ringing to say he enjoyed the commentary somehow and sure enough. Gordon felt I was hinting they were arrogant. I certainly never meant it that way, far from it, but we begged to differ.

Gordon was one of those managers I had been ringing for team news and I quite enjoyed speaking to him but I thought it was best to take a breather on that. He always made me laugh by saying being an Old Firm manager is harder than being Prime Minister. That may not be the case but they're probably on a level pegging!

Things were a little frosty for a while although I always made a point of congratulating Gordon when he won a trophy because I thought his record at Celtic was rather impressive.

He's now totally transformed the national team too and Scotland have given themselves a great chance of making it to Euro 2016 in France. I so hope they do. It's been an awful long wait since their last major tournaments the 1998 World Cup, which was also in France. That must be an omen! Let's believe.

There's a feelgood factor about Scotland these days and the team are performing admirably under Strachan but if they ever do have an off-day while I'm commentating I don't think I'll ever say they were put in their place.

Strachan's successor was Tony Mowbray who'd stitched me up when he was Hibs manager once by giving me a duff formation which then went out live on TV. Alas he chose a day to do it when his team were 2-0 down early on. I couldn't resist a 'maybe he told the players the wrong formation too'.

Tony's Hibs team were a really good watch – they even put Celtic in their place once! But Tony would never offer much help when it came to giving out his team. He just didn't see the point. He asked me to explain why I needed such information one day so I did explain in detailed fashion and at the end he still said, 'No I don't get it.'

I quite liked him though. He had a dry sense of humour which appealed to me. I'm surprised it didn't work out too well for him at Celtic. I thought it would. Another pish prediction on my part!

Tony never looked like he was ever enjoying the Celtic job. I remember chatting to him in the tunnel before a match at Motherwell and he seemed particularly downbeat. I thought, 'Blimey, he's going to have to go in that dressing room and inspire the players soon.'

Tony had played for Celtic so must have known what to expect but I just don't think the job was for him sadly. He was also travelling between his family in the Midlands and Scotland which wasn't ideal. I was doing the same but I wasn't managing Celtic. I think you have to be there all the time, preferably with a wee escape abode in the marvellous Scottish countryside!

Neil Lennon took over for his first managerial posting but he was hardly going to be a John Barnes. He knew Celtic inside out having been there as a player for so long and then returning as a coach. After a testing start (I think that goes with the territory) Lenny grew into the job despite having to put up with some horrendous nonsense like when that idiot attacked him at Tynecastle.

Lenny was often portrayed as some sort of thug himself yet he is one of the most interesting and intellectual guys I've come across in the game. You only have to listen to him when he's a pundit on TV. Listen and learn.

I hope he does well at Bolton although after what he ultimately achieved at Celtic I thought he might have done a bit better than Bolton. Don't get me wrong, they're a smashing club, but they've been in better positions than now. Having said that, it wouldn't surprise me if Lenny brought them back to those better positions.

I also hope Alex McLeish finds a way back into the British game as he has a lot more to offer than many seem to think. His record is pretty impressive but he's still paying for one or two downturns in his career.

Blimey it's harsh out there. It's dog eat dog and manager eat manager!

When I commentated on the Championship nearly all of the managers would give me their teams well in advance every single time. I'd worked at it though by visiting training grounds and getting to know them a bit better away from the pressures of a matchday. It was an easier environment to explain what I needed and to build up trust. I could ring 22 of the 24 managers and get their teams immediately and I respect them all for that. You want to know who the two are don't you?

Glenn Hoddle was a bit cagey at Wolves although he did relent once and along with Chris Kamara we had a cuppa and a chat in his office at Molineux. That was quite fascinating too. I suppose any former England manager would be a bit cagey come to think of it. It would've been interesting to see where Glenn might have taken England had he stayed in charge.

Craig Levein had been fine to deal with at Hearts but he was a little harder to get hold of when he landed the Leicester City job. I remember him having a pop at me one day, moaning that I'd been hounding him. This was technically true. I'd rung him six times and left two messages. Well, try answering the phone or returning my call then!

After Craig left Leicester he worked with us on a Hearts v Barcelona friendly and sidled up to me before the game saying he'd got an early shout on the Hearts team and how useful it was to know in advance. Yes indeed, exactly my bloody point!

I used to love ringing Neil Warnock at Sheffield United and my favourite call to him was when I woke him up one late afternoon ahead of an evening game. 'You've just woken me up. F*** off.' He usually got straight to the point did Neil. He slammed the phone down but when I saw him a couple of hours later he was particularly pleasant, as if he never remembered the call. Maybe he thought it was a dream.

I got on well with his assistant Kevin Blackwell, who later became a manager himself. When Sheffield United reached the play-off final in 2003 they took the players away to a hotel near where I lived. I met up with Kevin for a coffee and he gave me the team for the final, eight days before the actual game. That might just be the earliest I've ever had a line-up!

When Kevin was in charge of Leeds United I used to pop into his office for a cuppa before matches. One day his office was bustling with his friends and family and Kevin appeared a bit preoccupied so I took that as a hint to get out his way. As I walked out of his office who should I immediately bump into in the Elland Road tunnel? Kevin Blackwell.

I'd just been trying to get some team news out of his twin brother in the office. I'm telling you, the likeness in looks and voice was uncanny!

I went to interview Bryan Robson at Middlesbrough one day and he kept us waiting for two hours due to an unforeseen pressing issue he had to deal with. Cameraman Dave Caine and I sat in a suite at the Riverside watching heavy snow come down as we waited and waited and waited.

Dave said the worst thing was Bryan would come in and say, 'Sorry to keep you waiting lads,' and we would both go, 'That's okay, no problem,' as if we liked hanging around for bloody hours being bored to bits. Bryan did just that but I promptly burst out laughing as he said it and got the major giggles. I could barely compose myself to actually interview him. He did ask what the joke was but we couldn't tell him!

Ade Akinbiyi kept me waiting for two and a half hours for an interview at Leicester's training ground once so at least Bryan was lagging behind him. Ade wasn't worth the wait though, at least Bryan was. Just!

The first manager I ever interviewed was George Graham at Arsenal. It just had to be a Scot. He was a bit scary to be honest but then I was a bit scared as it was my first time. I've crossed the path of a few managers since then. It was fascinating to spend a little time with the likes of Sir Bobby Robson, Dario Gradi and Joe Royle.

I'm not in awe of many people but I pretty much was with Sir Bobby. I don't know why. He wouldn't have wanted you to be in awe but there was just something about him. He remains the only manager I've only had to ask one question to in a post-match interview.

'What's your overall verdict on the game Sir Bobby?' As he started his reply I began thinking of my next few questions but then he quickly covered everything I would've been asking. And he just carried on and on, covering every single talking point in the match. When he finally stopped four minutes later I just added, 'Er, thanks Sir Bobby.' He was some man.

I had a cup of coffee with Dario in his office at Crewe's training ground. Twenty minutes listening to that man was an education and a half in all things football but especially in the development of an academy, a club and a philosophy.

Joe was brilliant to deal with and has my favourite type of sense of humour, dry! He would always invite you into his office after a game for a cup or glass of something. He was Ipswich manager when they were involved in an epic play-off semi-final with West Ham. Ipswich had won the first leg 1-0 but West Ham won the second leg 2-0 on a night when Upton Park was at its very best for atmosphere.

I would've loved to have seen Joe in the final, if he hadn't been facing the Hammers. He was so immensely likeable I might have even accepted a West Ham defeat on this occasion. But then I remembered Joe was in charge of that Oldham team on the night of that Valentine's Day Massacre in the torrential rain in 1990. Six bloody nil. Sorry Joe, payback time!

Of the current crop of managers Alan Pardew, Steve Bruce and Tony Pulis are always a joy to deal with. There's a lot to be said for experienced managers but I also like to spot early potential in the younger ones.

A few years ago I was doing Burnley when Eddie Howe was their manager. I didn't know Eddie so rang him up and asked if it would be possible to have a chat for ten minutes at the ground before the game. He was very obliging and helpful and I thought at the time he had something about him, despite his tender age.

Some managers just have a certain thing about them and a presence, an aura. I know that's a rubbish explanation but it's actually so hard to explain. I know it when I see it and, unusually for me, I've rarely been proved wrong in that respect.

Karl Robinson is another in the Howe mould. I covered MK Dons a few times and left feeling like Karl was my best mate. I also liked the fact that he told his players to remove headphones and not use their mobiles when arriving at away grounds and walking through to the dressing rooms. Instead he had all of them saying hello to everyone. There's a lot to be said for such basic courtesy in football.

Eddie has now reached the Premier League with Bournemouth which is a remarkable story. And Karl has taken MK Dons into the Championship after some play-off disappointments. I shall be watching with interest. These guys are going to the top.

Alex Neil is another who has that look about him. He took Norwich City into the top flight of England football 12 months after taking Hamilton Accies into the top flight of Scottish football. It's about time the Premier League had another Scottish manager. There were several not so long ago but they all seemed to fall by the wayside rather hastily. It's time to go again Scotland!

Alex started the 2014/15 season by overseeing a Hamilton game that attracted 730 fans. He ended the season by winning the Championship play-off final in front of 85,000 at Wembley and a worldwide audience of millions.

Next stop Old Trafford, The Emirates, The Etihad and Stamford Bridge. Talk about taking the fast track. The good thing about Alex is that, although I somehow doubt he'll be missing New Douglas Park (the red bus parked behind the goal is wonderfully quaint mind you), he will never forget the place or the people.

14

Toilet Rolls and Townships

MY first experience of a major international tournament was the World Cup in 1994. We weren't actually commentating for Capital Radio but they had agreed a sponsorship deal where we could report on the games and gather interviews.

The tournament was held in the USA and was an incredible experience. I was to spend a couple of weeks in New York and Boston and the latter end of the tournament in Los Angeles. Well okay, if you insist.

Although it was a little scary at times. I had to feed the interviews back to Capital in London from an apartment owned by a journalist who had the necessary technical equipment to do just that. It didn't look like the safest part of town.

After evening matches it would be 2am before I would leave that apartment on my own. I can still hear him closing the locks on his front door. There must have been eight of them being slammed shut as I ventured out on to the streets of Iffyville. I may as well have stuck a big target sign on my backside. It was an immense relief when a taxi stopped and I was able to escape.

I loved New York though. I went back in 2008 and got engaged there. That fantastic city had obviously been through such a lot in the intervening years and it felt safer and even better than in 1994. A city to inspire. I think I could happily live there although commuting to Kilmarnock and Dingwall might be an issue.

I digress. Among the matches I reported on in 1994 was Bulgaria's shock win over Germany in the quarter-finals. We had access to what is called the mixed zone after the match, where players walk through to be interviewed by the world's media, if they agreed. They often didn't.

Most of the media had been attracted to one of the Bulgarian heroes, Yordan Letchkov, when suddenly Lothar Matthaus came into my vision. It was just him and me. My big chance! To this day

I'm still surprised I actually said boldly, 'Lothar…a quick word for Capital Radio London?' The look on his face made the Fergie Stare appear a warm welcoming smile. Well, if you don't ask. On reflection I probably shouldn't have.

I saw Italy v Spain in Boston, a beautiful city and at that game at the Foxborough Stadium I got to meet the legendary ITV commentator Brian Moore. He was working with Ron Atkinson, who I knew by that time via my radio work in Birmingham. Big Ron introduced me to Brian, one of the voices of my childhood. It's always nice when those you admire turn out to be really good guys and Brian was just that. A pleasant, humble, genuine man and what an operator.

I wasn't working on the final between Brazil and Italy at the Pasadena Rosebowl in Los Angeles but I was determined to go to the game. I hadn't come all this way to not go to a World Cup Final. I was thinking I may never get to another. And I haven't!

I wangled a ticket and sat next to a couple of Dutchmen and a Norwegian family in the searing Californian heat. Brazil and Italy duly bored us to bits for 120 minutes before Brazil won on penalties. But hey, it was a World Cup Final and I was there. I took a picture as Roberto Baggio missed the decisive penalty and the Brazilian players went crazy around him as he hung his head. The agony and the ecstasy of football, on the biggest stage of all. Those are the games of our lives.

Two years later I was part of the Capital Radio team covering the 1996 European Championships which were held in England. In a sign of things to come I was covering Scotland at Villa Park on the night they faced Switzerland and England met Holland at Wembley.

Terry Venables's team certainly turned on the style that night, thrashing the Dutch 4-1. Scotland were pretty good too. They battered the Swiss but with only an Ally McCoist goal to show for it. Typically that solitary Dutch goal was enough to put them through and send Scotland out. The Scots should've won by four or five but it wasn't their first hard luck story. Or their last.

Scotland are absolute masters of a nearly-but-not-quite moment. They lost to England in a play-off for Euro 2000 yet won the Wembley leg and gave their Auld Enemy a huge scare in doing so. They could easily have been victorious overall.

A 2002 World Cup qualifier against Belgium summed them up perfectly. Billy Dodds put them ahead in the second minute. Start as you mean to go on. Eric Deflandre was sent-off for handling on the line and Dodds scored the penalty. It was 2-0 against ten men. What could possibly go wrong?

Barry Ferguson had a great chance to make it 3-0. He didn't. Marc Wilmots got one back for Belgium early in the second half and wouldn't you just know, Daniel van Buyten rose in stoppage time to equalise.

I really felt for Craig Brown and Scotland on that day in particular. It was such a crushing blow. Van Buyten went on to have a great career but whenever I heard his name it was a bit like hearing George Reilly's name. He scored that FA Cup winner for Cambridge bloody United against Weymouth.

I had an affinity with the Scottish national team from my early days of covering them to this very day. Some narrow-minded folk used to slaughter me purely for being an Englishman daring to commentate on Scotland. If you think I'm a crap commentator that's fine but there's not much I can do about being English. I was born with it.

To be honest I would rather watch Scotland than England now and I do love a bit of 'Flower of Scotland' to get me going. Then I'll join in with anything from The Proclaimers and also 'On the Bonny Bonny Banks of Loch Lomond' which is often played at half-time at Hampden Park. I can't get enough of that song. I've even got it on iTunes! I'm sure I'm transforming into a Scot.

In the first leg of a play-off for Euro 2004 Scotland stunned Holland 1-0 at Hampden Park. Former Rangers boss Dick Advocaat was in charge of the Dutch and I saw him in the Hampden tunnel after the game. 'It's not a problem Ian, we will absolutely batter them in Amsterdam.' Dick was right and Holland won 6-0.

In the 2006 World Cup qualifiers Scotland drew with Slovenia and Moldova and lost to Norway in their first three matches. Over before it started.

It was a different story for Euro 2008 though. Scotland were drawn with world champions Italy and the French. They couldn't have picked a harder group yet under Walter Smith and then Alex McLeish Scotland pushed them all the way.

Amazingly they beat France twice but a horrible defeat in Georgia in the penultimate match meant they needed a result against Italy in the final game.

Typically Scotland found themselves behind when Luca Toni scored in the second minute. Barry Ferguson equalised but Christian Panucci grabbed an injury-time winner. How very Scotland. How very close. Close but no cigar. Just a fag end as usual.

Norway pipped the Scots to the runners-up spot for a place at the 2010 World Cup. Scotland started that campaign with a 1-0 defeat in Macedonia where the September weather topped 104 degrees. I normally like a bit of sunshine in a stadium but it was just too bloody hot in Skopje. That was definitely the sweatiest I've ever been at a football match. I think Scotland would have been better served going there in winter.

Craig Levein was in charge for the Euro 2012 qualifiers and baffled the nation when he decided against playing with a striker in the Czech Republic. It was the 4-6-0 formation that Barcelona would come to use but with respect to Scotland that's got a better chance of working if you're Barcelona.

The Czechs had just lost at home to Lithuania and the natives were restless. They couldn't believe their luck at the lack of a Scottish striker though. The Czechs won 1-0 and those three points would prove decisive in them clinching the runners-up spot.

In 2006 I had made the difficult decision to leave Sky Sports for the newly formed Setanta Sports who had gained some Premier League rights. There were four pretty decent commentators ahead of me at Sky and I couldn't really argue with that, although I suspect the management will claim I tried to!

I was supposed to be the number one commentator on the Premier League for Setanta but then they changed their management structure and the new gaffer preferred someone else. Now I knew how footballers felt when a new boss came in and didn't fancy them! That's football. That's telly.

Switching to Setanta seemed like a good idea at the time but turned out to be the daftest decision I'd ever made. They went bust in 2008. After their demise I was working as a freelancer and in 2010 ITV Sport gave me the opportunity to go to the World Cup in South Africa. I was based mostly in Johannesburg. This was going to be an experience for sure!

I covered Argentina's opening game at Ellis Park. They only beat Nigeria 1-0 but it was a privilege to commentate on the likes of Messi, Di Maria, Veron and Tevez. I quickly decided Argentina were going to win the World Cup. They were thrashed by Germany in the quarter-finals. My predictions often turn out like that.

I also did Spain's opening game where they somehow contrived to lose to Switzerland. That was an extraordinary result because Spain played no different to usual. They just had one of those days in front of goal. How reassuring that it can happen to the very best. They may have lost their first match in the tournament but they won their last, the World Cup Final. Did anyone really doubt as much despite that initial setback?

Another stand-out match for me was Portugal 7 North Korea 0. Seven different scorers and it took the last of them, Cristiano Ronaldo, until the 87th minute to score the seventh! What kept him?

ITV had hired an apartment for their staff and I shared a flat with Chris Coleman, now Wales manager, who was working as a studio guest and commentator. I'd interviewed him a couple of times but didn't know him that well. No worries. After a couple of hours in Chris's company you feel like he's your best mate.

Chris brought a fair supply of red wine for our flat (fine by me) but then had to go away for a few days covering games. A night out in Johannesburg didn't look the safest idea so I often stayed in the flat alone.

His bottles of red wine never stood a chance. He did me hook line and sinker on his return. He rang saying, 'Crocks, I'm back at the flat, we've been burgled. Somebody's stolen all the wine.' I actually believed him at first!

We went to the local shop together once, a ten-minute walk from the flat. We were told not to go any further as there was a township nearby and it was best not to get ourselves noticed. Having loaded up with shopping we decided to get a taxi back. But could we find one?

One driver ended up ferrying us around for 20 minutes and then dumped us in the middle of nowhere, though thankfully not quite in the township. What a sight we must've been. And what potential targets.

I had visions of a TV news bulletin saying, 'Coleman was last seen clutching three bags of shopping, some red wine and a multi-pack of toilet rolls.' It was such a relief to eventually find a taxi driver who knew where he was going and it wasn't to the township.

One night we decided to risk the great Johannesburg outdoors and walked to a local bar. There were a few undesirables knocking about and it felt far from safe on the short walk. Chris turned to me and said, 'I want you to know if anything happens I'm running as fast as I can and leaving you to it.' Funny man. Although I doubt he was joking!

On my last night in South Africa one of the ITV security guys told me some stories. They'd been doing some work in another country a year earlier when one of their colleagues had stopped at traffic lights in scorching heat. His arm was resting on the open window and someone came by and chopped his arm off just to steal his watch. I'm glad the security guy saved that story for the last night. Even though it was in another country, I wouldn't have wanted to hear it on my first night.

South Africa did a great job of hosting the World Cup but I can't pretend I ever felt massively safe there. Sadly I never got to Cape Town which I've heard is fantastic. I won't be rushing back to Johannesburg but hey, many will be. It's a game of opinions. I'm glad I went and experiencing only my second World Cup was a memory to treasure. The ITV boys were a good bunch.

Years ago I covered the Copa America, South America's equivalent of the European Championships. It's always good if you get the Brazil or Argentina gig in that tournament but I ended up with Paraguay against Venezuela one night. Lucky me. On this occasion we were commentating off-tube from London so I was sat in front of a big telly which always makes it a bit harder to spot offsides or disallowed goals or other incidents.

The local TV coverage of the game was a bit ropey and the match director in South America kept flying off to shots of this and that and everything. Eight minutes into the second half he cut to one of the Paraguay players who was off the field by the dugouts looking all sweaty and unhappy.

I assumed they had made a substitution which the director had missed but as I started saying that they flashed a graphic over this player saying 'RED CARD'. Oh no! They never showed a replay to offer an explanation for the sending off and to this day I have no idea about it. I didn't ever want to know after a painful couple of minutes of commentating that felt like an hour. Sometimes digging yourself out of a big hole like that is nigh-on impossible.

I do remember turning to my co-commentator Mark Lawrenson and asking if he'd seen the incident, at which point we both fell about on the floor laughing.

I covered a youth tournament once involving England, Germany, Spain and Holland. Germany were beating England in the final game which meant they would win the tournament. Or so we thought. Having spent most of the afternoon saying how typical it was that the Germans were going to win this the organisers belatedly informed us that the results against the bottom team in the group wouldn't be counted.

This actually meant that Spain would win the tournament and not the Germans! I could have done with that information before the game. I can understand such a rule when you have the likes of San Marino or the Faroes in a qualifying group but not in a youth tournament like this with four decent footballing nations. I screeched into reverse gear in the commentary with just a couple of minutes remaining, having spent a good hour or so hailing Germany's triumph!

The Spanish players were actually sat in the stadium watching the final game but I don't think the baffling rule change had filtered down to them. On the full-time whistle Germany celebrated as if they had won it and the Spanish sat there as if they hadn't. Then the message got through and the roles were reversed. At moments like that there's only one thing you can do as a commentator. Hand back to the presenter quick and leave him to clear up the mess! It just goes to prove at the end of the day Germany actually don't always win!

Another international gig as a freelancer took me to Doha in Qatar for a friendly between Brazil and England in 2009. Amid much controversy Qatar has been awarded the World Cup in 2022 and it will certainly be interesting to see how that materialises. It seems it will be held in winter although this game was in November and it was still bloody boiling.

I've never been a great fan of friendlies but it was Brazil and England after all. I've done worse. And it was in the sunshine. Although the game still turned out like most friendlies, largely uneventful. My overriding memories of that trip were away from the football.

A truly magnificent chicken biryani in Qatar Airways's business class plus a non-stop supply of red wine. A five-star hotel in Doha which could easily have been rated ten-star. A Thai massage that was positively heavenly. I did a bit of prep for the game and then spent hours around the hotel pool or on the beach. Then I took the rest of my prep with me to do on the beach! I came back with a tan Phil Brown would've been proud of.

Hey, it's a tough job, but somebody's got to do it.

15

Had Mic Did Travel

MY random ramblings will soon be over which may come as a relief to some. Thanks for sticking with it this far, you're nearly done. Much of the remainder of this book takes you through the 2014/15 season and everything it entailed for a commentator like me. I hope I've taken you inside the world of a football commentator and a football fan, although most of you know what the latter is like if not the former.

Mind you there are far more commentators around than ever before these days. Times have changed. When I was young John Motson, Barry Davies and Brian Moore were the main men and televised football was in its infancy.

Now there are so many more games and so many more voices. Some of us do it one way, some of us do it another way but hey, if we all sounded the same it would be a tad dull.

As I think Barry Davies once said, 'One man's commentator is another man's pain in the arse.' So true and never ask a commentator for an opinion about another commentator. We're the absolute worst on that front, probably because we want to be doing the games they're doing!

Generally though there is a fair amount of respect and a tremendous camaraderie in the commentating industry because we all know it's not as easy as people think. Or as easy as we make it look! Honest! If indeed industry is the right word. I mean, it's hardly a proper job.

You don't realise how lucky you are. That's a line I've heard a few times over the years, usually from football fans who would dearly love to have a job like mine. You're all wrong. I do realise how lucky I am and I've never met a fellow commentator who doesn't think the same. Travelling the country and sometimes the world to watch football and getting paid for it. Come on, we know we're damn lucky!

One Christmas Day night I drove Craig Burley from the East Midlands to Scotland for an early Boxing Day kick-off. Burley, also known as 'The World's Worst Passenger', never shut up moaning about my driving and in frighteningly heavy fog on the A66 proclaimed, 'Just go for it, there'll be nobody around on Christmas night.' I so thought that could be his epitaph. And mine. The lucky part on this occasion was actually completing the journey in one piece. I've been campaigning for ejector seats in cars ever since.

I've known Craig since he was a young player at Chelsea. He's never been afraid to speak his mind and that's more than half the trick for a pundit. He was one of many excellent co-commentators I've worked with; the likes of Bobby Moore, Frank McLintock, Davie Provan, Chris Kamara, Alvin Martin, Tony Gale, Garry Birtles, Ray Houghton, Andy Walker, Alan McInally, Trevor Francis and Stan Collymore.

I've worked with Davie Provan the most and nothing will ever top the day we were doing Scotland against San Marino. I'd arranged for the latter's media officer to give us the team and formation when they arrived at the stadium but I couldn't find him anywhere. Davie marched up to their coach with a pen and piece of paper and beckoned him to write down his team and formation. I think it got lost in translation because the coach signed his autograph and handed it back. I can still see the look on Davie's face today. I'm not sure he'd been waiting all his life for that autograph.

I worked with Stan briefly on talkSPORT and admired the amount of homework he did. He would have a line on every club in the land in case a fan from one of those clubs rang his phone-in. A far cry from a phone-in on another station where the presenter said, 'I don't know much about your team, I only watch Premier League.' How lazy can you get?

I keep in touch with almost every co-commentator I've ever worked with although I don't see Scott Booth from the Setanta days much. But then even if I did, I wouldn't be able to get a bloody word in with Boothy prattling on forever!

If I was obliged to name a commentating hero of mine I would go back to my youth to someone who quite a few of my age also seem to name as their number one. So apologies for being predictable but I used to listen to Peter Jones on the old *Sport on 2* on BBC Radio 2. Radio 5 was a few years away from being in existence back then. I used to take my portable radio to Weymouth matches at the old Rec and blast it out in the vicinity of whoever wanted to hear it and whoever didn't.

Peter's voice was immense, a master of his craft, but he wasn't alone. There was Bryon Butler, Peter Lorenzo and Larry Canning. Voices of my childhood that made such an impression, even though I initially wanted to work in newspapers, probably because then I never thought I could make it on to the radio. I don't think my voice had broken at that point mind.

If I was pushed to name my favourite commentator of the modern era I would have to say myself. Ha, I'm joking there. It would probably be Rob Hawthorne because he's a good mate as well. Although Alan Parry's voice always gets me going but that's because I can still hear his radio commentary from the 1980 FA Cup Final when West Ham mauled Arsenal 1-0. It has kind of stuck with me. It's a bit sad that I can still repeat every word of it. At least I've never been sad enough to tell Alan as much!

Favourite stadium? A tough one. There's Glasgow, there's the Nou Camp, there's the San Siro. There's Upton Park, and the Recreation Ground at Weymouth for sentimental reasons. There's Anfield, Goodison Park and White Hart Lane for that proper-old-ground atmosphere. I love going to Newcastle and Sunderland. Giants Stadium in New York was fabulous. The Millennium Stadium in Cardiff when it hosted the Football League play-offs would be very high on my list.

But if I had to pick one I know which one it would be. I used to arrive there four or five hours before kick-off because you knew it was going to be busy but even by then the whole area around the ground was already packed and throbbing. I used to stand outside and people-watch for a while to feel the buzz, the passion, the excitement.

The behind-the-scenes staff at the club always had a touch of a class. Watching from the gantry always had the same effect on me as a commentator but also as a fanatical football follower. I loved it, especially the sheer enormity of the stadium and the sheer size of the club. You may have guessed. It's Old Trafford.

More people seem interested in what the worst ground is though. I have to say I love the ancient nature of Fratton Park, Portsmouth, and Pompey's terrific support, but the climb up the ladder to the top gantry there is scary. When you get to the top it's then quite a frightening stretch to get your feet across from the ladder to the actual gantry, which more often than not was covered with slippery pigeon shit. It was like an assault course. Oooh the glamour of it all.

In recent years they've moved the gantry down to a lower level, too low in fact because the view isn't great but at least you don't have to climb that bloody life-threatening ladder.

Talking of pigeon shit, a pigeon did shit on me once during a game at Gillingham. It was just after a goal had been scored so I'd obviously got a bit excited and maybe Mr Shitty Pigeon did too. Thanks a lot. I have viewed pigeons with suspicion ever since.

Gillingham was a nasty ladder climb to the gantry too, as was Grimsby, Cardiff and a good few others, even Everton! There was one ladder that stands out slightly more than Portsmouth and that was for a cup replay between Berwick Rangers and Rangers. We'd had to erect a serious amount of scaffolding to hold a television gantry at Shielfield Park because its facilities were rather limited as a lower league club.

The longest ladder in the world got you up there. Honestly, the *Guinness Book of World Records* might have been in attendance checking its validity. Naturally it was the night of a mini Berwick hurricane too and this ladder was swaying from side to side. It had passed the safety checks. It just didn't look like it had. I felt a sense of pride in climbing that ladder and reaching the top although not for long because I knew I still had to go back down it. You're only as good as your last ladder attempt.

I'm thinking Gayfield Park, Arbroath, might be the windiest place on earth. The gantry overlooks the North Sea and the first time I went there, for a cup game against Rangers, there was another near hurricane occurring. Funny how that seems to happen a lot on Scottish matchdays.

I was asked to wear a safety harness to avoid being blown into the aforementioned sea. I declined as I thought I would look a complete idiot wearing one of those. I decided it would have to be a major gust to blow a fat commentator into the sea but I tell you what, the major gusts in Arbroath were up for the challenge. I battled through bravely.

Several years later I returned to Arbroath for another cup game against Celtic on a rather cold and windy night. On arrival it was so blustery as I walked around the side of the pitch towards the dressing rooms I was beginning to wonder if I'd ever get there. I was being blown backwards. When I did get there a steward said, 'You're lucky, the wind has dropped a bit in the past hour.' You what?! I thought he was having a laugh but actually he wasn't.

I'm cold-weather-trained after 17 years working out and about in Scotland. I'm always prepared. That night I wore a thermal vest, shirt, pullover, two fleeces and a big double-lined Barbour jacket and I was absolutely frozen bloody stiff by 6.45pm. Not good when the kick-off wasn't until 7.45pm. Okay, I'm always prepared, apart from for Arbroath.

It nearly went to extra time and if it had done I would have needed chipping out of ice. My bones were still creaking and shuddering three days later. Ah well, enough of these fields of dreams.

I've nothing particularly against Grimsby Town or Norwich City but they do have something in common. I've been locked in at both grounds. Tom Ross's radio phone-in live from the game we had commentated on never used to finish until 7pm on a Saturday.

Most stadiums are still a bit busy by then but not Blundell Park. Everyone had buggered off home. We had to prise open a gate and squeeze through to escape. I think I was a bit thinner in those days. I'm not sure if we damaged the gate but let's face it, I can't imagine there were too many people trying to break in there.

At Carrow Road we shoved open a door on a fire escape which seemed like a good idea at the time but it set an alarm off. Ooops. We did the decent thing. We ran to the car and scarpered quickly. Sorry Norwich!

I would find it impossible to name my favourite player because I've seen a few over the years. Today it's Lionel Messi and Cristiano Ronaldo, and I think I would put them in that order. In that fabulous Manchester United team there was Beckham, Keane, Scholes and Giggs, and I could've mentioned that whole side. There was Henrik Larsson. But

I'm heading back to my childhood on this one. It would have to be Billy Bonds of West Ham or Anniello Iannone of Weymouth. I know, I'm going all sentimental now for sure.

Talking of sentimental, I was lucky enough to be able to tick the box on one of my ambitions.

The date was 14 November 2005.

Weymouth had held Nottingham Forest to a draw at the City Ground in the FA Cup. The replay was live on Sky Sports and I was hoping I would land it so I could commentate on my home-town team. I think I probably begged and pestered the management for it because sure enough it came my way.

I did a big interview in the *Dorset Evening Echo* on the day of the game about my time supporting the Terras as a boy and the memories of my best game ever, that remarkable FA Cup triumph against Cardiff City at Ninian Park.

Alas there was to be no repeat of such giantkilling heroics as Forest won 2-0 but no matter, I had got to commentate on Weymouth at the Wessex Stadium. It was a shame it wasn't at my and their old haunt, the Recreation Ground, but they had moved on from there.

Even so, it was a night to remember, a night that had me feeling like a teenager again, even though

I was 40! I felt like I'd gone full circle. From a fan at Cardiff v Weymouth to a commentator at Weymouth v Nottingham Forest.

It meant a lot to me to commentate on the Super Terras but every game counts for me. Sure, I've done loads of matches that on paper look like they could be stinkers and on grass turn out to be exactly that. You have to take the rough with the smooth. I don't think I'll ever lose the enthusiasm for the job. I understand why some commentators want to go on forever. Well, you would wouldn't you?

I did two games in one day once so I can hardly talk. The first was the chaos and mania of an Old Firm clash at lunchtime in front of a packed, snarling stadium. Then we drove to Perth for a rather more sedate affair between St Johnstone and Kilmarnock in front of one man and his dog. Funnily enough I remember the second match more even though it was utterly dire.

Saints boss Sandy Clark had told me before the game about one of his young players, Emmanuel Panther. High praise indeed. I gave him the big build-up as he prepared for a free kick in sight of goal. He then proceeded to somehow, against all odds, send the free kick out for a throw-in with one of the worst shots ever in the history of shots. I couldn't stop laughing for the rest of the game, not helped by the fact that nor could director Jerry Logan in my headphones.

After the match a few colleagues were waiting for me in a people carrier to return to Glasgow and as I got in the front seat I said, 'What a pile of shite that was,' only to get a clip round the ear because unbeknown to me we were giving Kilmarnock boss Bobby Williamson a lift. You couldn't make a day like that up.

I reached the big Hawaii Five O in 2015. Fifty years old. Was it really 35 years ago when West Ham last lifted the FA Cup? Was it really 33 years ago when Weymouth flayed the Welsh dragons of Cardiff? Was it really 29 years ago when I became stadium announcer at West Ham? Was it really 24 years ago when I did my first football commentary? Was it really 15 years ago when Celtic beat Rangers 6-2 and Hibs beat Hearts 6-2? Was it really five years ago when Motherwell and Hibs drew 6-6?

Time flies when you are having fun but there are things that still need to happen for me. I hope Weymouth make it into the Football League although it's going to take a while. I also hope West Ham win a trophy but if I had one wish relating to football it would be to have Hearts, Rangers and Hibs all back in the top flight of Scottish football. These are big clubs with followings to match and in my opinion we need them all up and at each other for the good of the Scottish game.

It despairs me to see swathes of empty seats at so many Scottish grounds, especially in a country where so many people are crying out for a bit of decent football. Maybe a 16-team or 18-team top league is the answer? Maybe summer football would help? That's an option I've never thought about seriously before but I'm starting to think it's not such a bad idea, especially if I ever have to go to Arbroath again. Although I bet it's blowing a bloody gale there in June too.

I also think it would be great if the Scottish play-off finals are one-off occasions as they are in England. I was lucky enough to commentate on a good few finals down south and they will remain extremely high on my list of career highlights, and not just because West Ham actually managed to win one of them.

We've all got our opinions but it's down to the Scottish clubs at the end of the day. It's up to them to decide whether it's time for change but I do think something needs to be done to shake up football in a country that I've grown rather fond of over the years, and not just when I spend a bit of time gazing out from those bonny bonny banks of Loch Lomond. Just beautiful. That's my favourite place but the rest of the country isn't too shabby either!

I'm so fond of Scotland I'm sneaking in a second wish. To see the national team qualify for a major tournament. It's been too long. Far too bloody long. As I've already mentioned in this book and frequently mention on air Scotland haven't qualified for a major tournament since 1998, the year I started commentating regularly on Scottish football. Although I did do an Aberdeen v Dunfermline play-off for Grampian Television in 1995, but back then I was just whetting my appetite.

Not only have the Tartan Army had to listen to an Englishman prattling on about their team for so long, they haven't been able to set up summer camp anywhere. Over to you Gordon, a nation expects, it's time for you to put others in their place!

There's always been a Scot on my career path so in terms of working in Scotland maybe some things were meant to be. They were usually the boss as well. Aren't they always?! There's even one in my life path. My wife Sharon was born in Dundee and she's definitely the boss.

From a broadcasting debut sat next to Ken Bruce on Radio 2, to Richard Park at Capital Radio in London, Tom Ross at BRMB Radio had Scottish connections, or should I say Celtic connections and then there were Aberdonians Colin Davidson and Andy Melvin at Sky Sports.

Andy usually kept things simple but effective in an Aberdonian kind of way. I've always remembered his regular sound advice when I went off to commentate on a game. 'Don't f*** up!' I did occasionally but hopefully I'm in credit and anyway shush, I won't tell anybody if you don't.

I have been classed as a jobbing commentator and that's probably fair enough. After all I have commentated on the Premier League, Football League Championship, League 1, League 2, Scottish Premiership, Scottish Championship, Scottish League One, Scottish League Two, FA Cup, English League Cup, Scottish Cup, Scottish League Cup, Champions League, UEFA Cup, Europa League, World Cup, European Championships, La Liga, Serie A, Copa del Rey, Coppa Italia, Bundesliga, Conference, Victory Shield, Intertoto Cup, Copa America, and FA Youth Cup. I may have missed a couple competitions along the way.

The job has taken me around England, Scotland, Wales, Northern Ireland and the Republic of Ireland and to the USA, South Africa, Spain, France, Germany, Italy, Portugal, Holland, Poland, Iceland, Turkey, Ukraine, Switzerland, Georgia, Denmark, Greece, Slovakia, Slovenia and

Macedonia. I may have missed a couple of countries along the way.

Jobbing it is then. That Scottish newspaper wasn't far off when it tagged me as a 'Have Mic Will Travel' commentator in 1998. Except that I never actually travelled with the mic. It was always just there when I turned up. The sound man had it all along. And isn't that just typical of sound men? Always there when you need them whether they're making you sound good or making the coffees!

I couldn't have done it without them or a good few others who've been there on a commentator's journey. Cheers all.

16

My Season in a Chapter

AUGUST

I start 2014/15 by sussing out Rangers. It's their final pre-season friendly before the big kick-off and they're at Derby County. It's a routine friendly yet amazingly it attracts 10,000 Rangers fans. I don't know why that still surprises me. I know how big a club they are. Those supporters have been to hell and back over the last few years yet they have been there every step of the way.

A week later I check out Hibs, whose on-loan goalkeeper Mark Oxley scores in a 2-1 win against Livingston. I've never witnessed a keeper doing that in person before so thanks Mark for allowing me to tick that off my list. It's a winning start for new

Hibs boss Alan Stubbs, one of the game's really good guys.

I walk from Easter Road to Edinburgh Waverley train station after the game in the pleasant sunshine but the streets were bulging with Edinburgh Festival goers. Not my scene when I'm working so time to head back to the gritty city of Glasgow.

My first commentary of the season is a 2-1 win for Hearts at Rangers. Hearts are under new management too with Robbie Neilson appointed head coach and Craig Levein as director of football. New owner Ann Budge had harshly sacked Gary Locke but by the end of the season her decision would be justified, although Gary might always think he could've done what Robbie did.

Much is made of the high proportion of kids in the Hearts squad but these are no ordinary kids. They've already got a lot of games under their belts. They're streetwise and they can play the game.

Next up Celtic win 3-0 at St Johnstone in their league opener but they're gifted two goals from defensive errors and a penalty as well. A false 3-0, rather like the one they were awarded a week earlier against Legia Warsaw.

Celtic were given a Champions League reprieve after the Poles were punished for fielding an ineligible player for a couple of minutes.

Harsh in the extreme as Legia had well and truly thumped Celtic across both legs. But rules are rules. It was nothing to do with Celtic and you can't turn down another crack at Europe's elite club competition.

Alas they failed miserably to make the most of their second chance, losing to Maribor. The first leg ended 1-1. I've never known Celtic Park as tense as it was on the night of that second leg against the Slovenian champions. It wasn't the Celtic Park I know on a big European night. A far cry from a year earlier when it was bouncing, shaking and jumping as Shakhtar Karagandy were disposed of amid a cacophony of noise.

Brazilian striker Tavares nabbed a late winner for Maribor. I was as frustrated and annoyed as anyone because the Champions League adventures were a highlight of the season. I consoled myself mildly by thinking how funny it is that every team in the world seems to have at least one Brazilian in their ranks. Wherever you go, that's a fact!

Also I kept thinking of the song 'Heaven Must be Missing an Angel' whenever I said Tavares's name. I would end up covering Maribor instead in the Champions League so was humming that bloody tune for a while. So, trust a Scottish club to be knocked out of the Champions League twice in a matter of weeks. Celtic Park fell horribly silent as Celtic fell into the Europa League.

New boss Ronny Deila was certainly finding the going tough and I thought Dundee United would give him a game. I bumped into United manager Jackie McNamara in a hotel the night before the game and he was thinking the same. What the heck do we know? Celtic won 6-1.

The Edinburgh derby. Well, at least that derby was still going! Can't live with each other, can't live without. Hearts' pain of relegation was eased a little when their city rivals only went and followed them down to the Championship after somehow contriving to lose a play-off to Hamilton Accies, even though they won the away leg 2-0. The fans were better than the game for a long time but Hearts ruled the capital again after a cracking goal from young Sam Nicholson got them going.

A taste of the English Premier League. Spurs thrash QPR 4-0 and Aston Villa beat Hull 2-1. I was chatting to Hull boss Steve Bruce before the game and he asked what I thought about Villa. I said I just didn't feel Gabby Agbonlahor and Andi Weimann scored enough goals. He retorted, 'You shouldn't have said that, they'll go and bloody score now.' They bloody did. Ooops! Sorry Brucey. I made sure I avoided him afterwards.

SEPTEMBER

An ambition realised, a first visit to the Westfalen Stadion in Dortmund. World champions Germany are rather fortunate to beat Scotland 2-1. Ikechi Anya scores the goal of his dreams to equalise but Germany grab a scruffy winner. Anya makes everyone laugh by saying he couldn't score past Manuel Neuer on FIFA but now he'd done it in real life.

I stayed in a hotel that made it into my top three of horrible hotels. The other two were in Donetsk and Grimsby. It was previously called the Unique Hotel and still had the old illuminated sign up, except the letters 'que' were missing. Maybe that was what made it unique. Or should I say uni?

I commentate on Cyprus's first competitive away win for seven years. It comes in Bosnia and Herzegovina after Edin Dzeko squanders a stack of chances. 'These misses could prove so costly,' I say. Hardly rocket science I know but nice to be proved right for a change.

I think Aberdeen could worry Celtic on their trek to Glasgow but the champions score at the start of each half and even though Aberdeen pull one back they're beaten 2-1. That was a sign of things to come between those two teams.

The Scottish champions may not have made it into the Champions League but thankfully I'd hung in there. I saw Carlos Tevez make the difference as Juventus beat Malmo and it appears I'm the new Maribor correspondent. Well, at least I know them quite well by now. They equalise in stoppage time to draw with Sporting Lisbon.

Arsenal score three goals in as many first-half minutes at Aston Villa and Villa had arguably been the better team up until then. Villa had been hit by a flu bug and both teams settled for a 3-0 in a desperately dire second half. Arsene Wenger joked it looked like they had made an agreement at half-time to do no more. He might not have been joking actually. It really did look that way.

Two clubs, one street. I love the Dundee derby and we're a bit short of passionate derbies in Scotland at the moment. Dundee United stroll it 4-1 but I like the look of Dundee and in particular Greg Stewart, signed from Cowdenbeath. It's good to see players from the lower divisions given a chance and grasping that chance. We'll be seeing and hearing a lot more about Greg in the years to come methinks.

I see Celtic win 2-1 at struggling St Mirren before ending the month with my new pals Maribor who draw again, this time at Schalke. I admire their spirit but I just wish they were Celtic. Much more fun.

OCTOBER

I was looking forward to Atletico Madrid v Juventus but it doesn't live up to expectation. It was nowhere near as good as it should have been. How often is that the case with big matches?

Atletico edged it 1-0, such is their way.

Inverness Caledonian Thistle and Ross County share the honours in the Highland derby in front of a disappointing crowd. Caley Thistle might have to win the Champions League to get a few more punters through the door. Or maybe a Scottish Cup Final appearance might raise interest. I also see Ross County pumped 5-0 at home by Celtic.

I'm spending so much time in the Highlands I'm half expecting to bump into the Loch Ness Monster. Now that would be a story. I wouldn't mind being around if Nessie did put in an appearance. It would be up there with being able to commentate on Hibs winning the Scottish Cup.

I see Liechtenstein gain a rare point in the Euro qualifiers in a goalless draw with Montenegro, who battered them but couldn't score.

Scotland have got Georgia on their mind at Ibrox. I wonder how many times that line has been used in the media about Georgia. I'm pretty sure I've done it myself a few times. Scotland needed an own goal to get Georgia off their mind and then we all headed for Poland.

A first visit to Warsaw and I quickly decided I liked the place, although I ate Italian food on both nights I was there for some reason. Ah well, when in Warsaw.

Poland take an early lead but Shaun Maloney and Steven Naismith put the Scots 2-1 up amid an outstanding atmosphere. The Tartan Army give it large. Mind you, they always do, win, lose or draw! The Poles equalise and finish so strongly I suspect Gordon Strachan will take a 2-2. Not that I would dare ever speak on Gordon's behalf. At least they weren't put in their place!

Schalke beat Sporting Lisbon 4-3 in a Champions League thriller but the winning goal is a penalty for a handball that never was. The assistant behind the goal really should have spotted as much. How many officials do they need? Although of course video technology is the real answer.

Juventus disappoint again, losing 1-0 at Olympiakos. The Old Lady of Italian football sometimes look like old ladies plodding through the group stage. Talk about making hard work of it but that seems to be an Italian thing when it comes to the groups, at club and international level.

I end the month at West Brom 2 Crystal Palace 2, a lively encounter but neither manager Alan Irvine nor Neil Warnock would be hanging around for long.

NOVEMBER

I love it when you see someone who makes you think, 'Bloody hell, you are good.' My mouth waters watching Alexis Sanchez as Arsenal beat Burnley 3-0. What a sensational player. His workrate is an example to many. They say it comes from the time he played street football growing up in Chile. They must have been fiercely contested mean streets!

Juventus come from behind to beat Olympiakos 3-2 in Turin. Fittingly, Andrea Pirlo floats in a free kick in his 100th Champions League match. Rather like Nakamura's title-clinching free kick at Kilmarnock, I just knew Pirlo was going to do that. I was able to give it the big build-up and then milk it afterwards. Grazie Andrea you absolute legend. I was reading his autobiography at the time. What a book. What a player. What a guy.

Sporting beat Schalke 4-2 in their return clash which would've made up for that dodgy penalty in Gelsenkirchen but Sporting failed to make the knockout stage and Schalke did so not much there in the way of a payback or consolation. I thought Sporting were better than Schalke too.

Virgil van Dijk scores a last-minute winner for Celtic at Aberdeen and after Scott Brown had been sent off too. It had taken Celtic until that point of the season to reach the top of the table. Aberdeen would later shunt them off again but getting the better of Celtic when they were on the same field was becoming a problem.

Celtic Park is once again throbbing under the lights as Scotland face the Republic of Ireland. Martin O'Neill is back on familiar territory but then so is Gordon Strachan. Shaun Maloney scores a wonderful winner, similar to a beauty he scored for Wigan against Manchester United. I had commentated on that goal too. Shame I didn't remember how similar it was until afterwards. Too late to say as much on-air.

Alan Pardew is enjoying a winning streak which continues as Newcastle beat QPR but he's not getting too carried. That club is always one defeat away from disarray.

About time I did Maribor, who lose 3-1 at Sporting. About time I did Juventus, 2-0 winners at Malmo.

I've not seen much of Motherwell so go to watch them lose 2-1 to Dundee United in the Scottish

Cup. After some exceptional seasons punching above their weight under Stuart McCall it's sad to see 'Well looking rather unwell.

I look forward to Hearts v Celtic in the Scottish Cup but Morgaro Gomis gets an early red card to kill the tie. Celtic cruise it 4-0.

DECEMBER

I admire Burnley's spirit in a 1-1 draw with Newcastle and drive slowly out of town. Ten years ago I reached 12 points for a minor speeding offence when leaving Turf Moor one night. I ended up in Burnley Magistrates' Court next to a load of suspected drug dealers after a police swoop the night before.

It was an interesting experience but not one I would wish to repeat.

Celtic score early at Motherwell but it isn't a sign of things to come this time. It ends 1-0. You always feel a bit cheated when you get an early goal and then that's it, there aren't any more.

Juventus need to avoid defeat at home to Atletico Madrid to reach the knockout phase of the Champions League. A drab goalless draw seems to suit both teams. I do Maribor for the final time as they lose to Schalke. See ya Maribor and next time please let Celtic through.

Manchester City are short of strikers but no worries, they have Frank Lampard who scores the winner at Leicester. I felt the Foxes deserved more out of the game. I'd be saying that for the next few months.

I'm reminded how good a ground Villa Park is and how good an atmosphere it generates when Villa take the lead against Manchester United. It finishes 1-1 but I was there when Villa scored. They failed to in their next six Premier League matches.

I see Rafa Benitez and Napoli win the Italian Super Cup, beating Juventus on penalties. The game was staged in Doha and it actually looked like both teams had agreed on a bit of shoot-out entertainment as part of the money-spinning deal to go to Qatar.

I feel for Alan Irvine, a good man, as Manchester City win at West Brom on Boxing Day. He wouldn't see the year out. A Boxing Day night flight to Edinburgh to see Hibs wallop a woeful Rangers 4-0 is followed by a quick return to Birmingham to see Aston Villa 0 Sunderland 0, 90 minutes of my life I won't ever get back or hopefully ever remember. It was a form of torture.

JANUARY

Happy Hogmanay. Not. Partick Thistle v Celtic is

postponed due to a waterlogged pitch. It rains a lot in Glasgow, surely we should be able to cope. No such worries on Kilmarnock's artificial pitch where Celtic win 2-0. I don't like the look of the artificial pitches but understand that for some clubs it's a case of needs must.

A friendly welcome as usual at Leicester City whose behind-the-scenes staff are always cheerful, forever smiling. Virgin Trains staff are a bit like that. It's my ambition to meet a miserable employee. Leicester have been so unlucky they're fast becoming my second team (or third behind Weymouth and West Ham) but they beat Aston Villa 1-0 and it could have been five or six.

Not for the first time in my life I appear to be stalking Celtic who win 2-0 at Hamilton and 1-0 at Ross County, who may have lost but who have improved under Jim McIntyre and Billy Dodds, two great guys.

It's good to catch up with Tony Pulis at West Brom but they're tonked 3-0 by Spurs. A reminder of the work still to be done by Tony but he'll do it. He does what it says on his relegation-avoiding tin.

FEBRUARY

Fiorentina leave it late to knock Roma out of the Coppa Italia. It's a largely incident-free tie but at least they spared us extra time. Napoli v Inter is a similarly grim encounter but Gonzalo Higuain scores a 93rd-minute winner for Napoli to spare us extra time again. God bless you Gonzalo.

Celtic score after seven minutes in the Scottish Cup at Dundee. Game over. Celtic score in the first minute at Partick Thistle in the league. Game over. Celtic score in the first minute again at St Johnstone. Game over. It would be nice to have a right good contest to commentate on.

Shakhtar Donetsk hold Bayern Munich to a 0-0 in an uninspiring affair. Bayern had scored eight goals against Hamburg in their previous game so had obviously used up all their goals.

Juventus 2 Dortmund 1 is much better. I've seen so much of Juve this season and there's so much to admire. Pirlo, Pogba, Tevez, Marchisio, Morata and of course Buffon. How good does that fella look? It's hard not to feel a bit of man love.

I see Paul Lambert's last game as Villa manager, a 2-0 defeat at Hull. I see Tim Sherwood's first game as Villa manager, a 2-1 defeat to Stoke. I feel for Paul, who looked a beaten man before the game at the KC Stadium. I feel for Tim, who gets a response from the players before a last-minute penalty kicks him in the teeth and possibly lower down the body. He'll dust himself down though, he's an infectious character. I worked with Tim at Setanta and he made me feel better about myself so I suspect he'll have a similar effect on footballers.

MARCH

Celtic thump their nearest challengers Aberdeen 4-0 in Glasgow. That's three wins out of three. Aberdeen have done so well to stay on Celtic's heels but the head-to-heads have ultimately made the difference.

I see Stoke beat Everton 2-0. I'm a big fan of Mark Hughes who mostly has an excellent record as manager. He could play a bit too! I've known Roberto Martinez since working with him on Spanish football years ago and when he played for Motherwell. Roberto's having a tough time but I'm sure he'll come through.

Funnily enough his Wigan and Everton teams always used to win when I was present. He thought I was a lucky omen. I made myself scarce after that defeat at Stoke!

Fiorentina end Juventus's 47-match unbeaten home run with a 2-1 win in the first leg of the Coppa Italia semi-final. Mo Salah, on loan from Chelsea, races up the pitch in Turin to score a stunner. He looked like he would score from the moment he set off.

Dundee United and Celtic draw 1-1 amid a flurry of red cards in the Scottish Cup. United's Paul Paton is sent off in a case of mistaken identity. I call it correctly much to my relief because there's always a moment in those kind of incidents when you think you've cocked it up rather than the ref. It was definitely the ref this time. Phew. Rather him than me. I told you the words 'commentator' and 'selfish' are never far away from each other.

Scottish referee Willie Collum sends off the right Shakhtar Donetsk man in the second minute in Munich. Bayern quickly become a great watch as they turn on the goal machine, winning 7-0.

Carlos Tevez inspires Juventus to a 3-0 win in Dortmund in what will be Jurgen Klopp's last season as Borussia boss. I hope he turns up in England. His press conferences could be a match for Jose's!

Newcastle are booed off at half-time at 2-0 down to Arsenal. They quickly get one back in a stirring second-half performance that has St James' Park jumping again. They deserve an equaliser but it doesn't come. Even so they are cheered off. Such is life up there.

Rangers buck the trend by beating Hibs for a change, winning 2-0 at Easter Road. It's the best I've seen Rangers in a long time. Stuart McCall has made an impression yet they can still be hit and miss.

I see Scotland edge Northern Ireland 1-0 in a friendly and then watch Austria thrash Liechtenstein 5-0. I seem to be seeing a lot of Liechtenstein. They're becoming my international Maribor!

Scotland are expected to thrash UEFA's newest arrivals, the part-timers of Gibraltar. Everyone else has. Gibraltar stay in the same hotel as me and seem a great bunch. I said to them before the game that if they were going to score their first competitive goal it would almost certainly be against Scotland.

They did and it was an equaliser from a policeman named Lee Casciaro but they are thrashed in the end, 6-1. Steven Fletcher scored the first Scotland hat-trick since Colin Stein in 1969. Forty-six years in the waiting. I'd been using the Stein line for 17 years but it was time to lay that stat to rest. It's like losing an old friend.

APRIL

Leicester were seven points from safety at the start of April but they are finally rewarded for their positive performances although their reward happens to come against my team West Ham. Wouldn't you just know it? Andy King scores a late winner at the

King Power and I'm not sure the atmosphere on the full-time whistle will be matched anywhere in the Premier League this season.

Dundee beat Dundee United for their first derby triumph in a decade, a testament to the fine work done by manager Paul Hartley at Dens Park, and they would later sneak into the top six before the split. Although don't get me started on that split!

Hibs beat Hearts for the first time this season but Hearts' work had long since been done. Having had a few pre-match cuppas with Alan Stubbs in his office, it's impossible not to like the guy. In fact there is man love potential although not quite on the same scale as Buffon!

Hibs dominate their Scottish Cup semi-final with Falkirk but just can't score. You know what's coming next. Craig Sibbald buries a late winner for Falkirk. That's football although Hibs must be kicking themselves. I have to double-check Craig is still only 19. I feel like I've been watching him for a while.

As I've detailed elsewhere in this book, Inverness stun Celtic 3-2 in the other semi-final which is clouded in controversy. I don't want to stoke that fire again here but John Hughes has done a colossal job at Caley Thistle. Terry Butcher had brought a lot of those players in and engrained them in spirit and character but Yogi soon stamped his mark on the club.

Many of those players were at lower league or even non-league clubs in England. Some were rejected by bigger clubs. There's something quite lovely about guys like that having their day in the sun. It helps you keep the faith in football.

West Brom 0 Liverpool 0 is barely worth this sentence. Dire. I shunt it out of my memory on the train to Scotland where Dundee United and Celtic meet for the 75th time in a fortnight or something like that. Leigh Griffiths excellently executes a Tannadice hat-trick, not long after also scoring a hat-trick against Kilmarnock. That boy can finish.

MAY

Dundee wave the white flag as Celtic thrash them 5-0, and the Hoops are confirmed as champions the next day when Aberdeen lose at Dundee United. It was always going to be a question of when not if but Aberdeen did push them all the way to May.

Hearts show the mark of champions by coming from 2-0 down to draw 2-2 with Rangers. They're then presented with the trophy. It'll be good to have them and those steep steps of Tynecastle back in the top flight. Outside of Glasgow there are few atmospheres to match that place.

In contrast, the KC Stadium is as flat as a pancake as Hull lose 1-0 at home to Burnley, who are relegated anyway as other results go against them. Burnley could be dragging Hull down with them at this rate. The Hull fans seem resigned to their fate. It's a good job the Leicester fans weren't.

I didn't realise Hull was quite so far from Aberdeen but after a long drive I see Celtic complete a season whitewash of the runners-up. They win 1-0 in an enjoyably feisty clash. There was nothing on it but the players didn't let that get in the way. A proper game.

Having seen so much of Leicester City I felt it was only right I should be there when they secured survival, and with a game to spare too. A 0-0 draw at Sunderland did the trick. You don't often get what you deserve in football but Leicester City and their fantastic fans certainly did.

Celtic lift the Scottish Premiership trophy after thumping Inverness 5-0 with a slick performance and some good goals but Caley Thistle had the Scottish Cup Final on their minds. I'm quite enthused by a Falkirk v Inverness final. It's quite refreshing.

Before the season is out I'll commentate on two teams for the first time, the nations of Qatar and Azerbaijan.

Then the full-time whistle goes on season 2014/15 after ten months of blood, sweat and tears and that was just me trying to get around the country. Although within a couple of weeks of the season ending you soon get bored and want it to start again. Okay, maybe that's within a couple of days really. Er, couple of hours anyone?

I suppose after 100 live commentaries it's time to take a breather but shall we do it all again in August? Yes please. Yes bloody please. In the meantime I've booked a wee summer break in Barcelona. I wonder if the missus will fancy a tour of the Nou Camp? Worth a try eh?